eavesdropping on MILLIONAIRES

eavesdropping
on
MILLIONAIRES

Investment Strategies and Advice
on How to
Build and Maintain Wealth

JOHN MAULDIN
& TIFFANI MAULDIN

WILEY

For general information on our other products and services or for technical support, please contact our Customer Care Department within the United States at (800) 762-2974, outside the United States at (317) 572-3993 or fax (317) 572-4002.

Wiley also publishes its books in a variety of electronic formats. Some content that appears in print may not be available in electronic formats. For more information about Wiley products, visit our web site at www.wiley.com.

Library of Congress Cataloging-in-Publication Data is Available:

ISBN 9781394194872 (Cloth)
ISBN 9781394194896 (ePDF)
ISBN 9781394194889 (ePUB)

Cover Art & Design: Paul McCarthy

SKY10054899_090723

For Pee-Paw and Papa Joe
& all those who came before
And for my Daddy
& all those who will come after

CONTENTS

The Creation Story of Eavesdropping On Millionaires

"Oh, that? I never thought it was eavesdropping, Aslan. Wasn't it magic?"

—C.S. Lewis, *The Voyage of the Dawn Treader*

Over a decade ago I sat up in bed after one of a handful of vivid dreams I've had in my life. I looked at the time on my pink Razr flip phone, and it was 2:37 a.m. Back then I was recording my dreams in the morning, and I had a yellow legal pad beside my bed.

I didn't dare turn on the light and risk the dream fading faster. I grabbed my pen and started writing. I knew (from past experience) that when writing in the dark, I would probably write over the same line more than once. So I wrote a few sentences and flipped the page. A sentence there, two words here, a few question marks, some seemingly outlandish words. Ten pages later, I went back to sleep.

The next morning, I awoke to over a dozen missed calls. My grandfather had passed away in the middle of the night during the surrounding moments I had been recording this download of a dream, June 21, 2007.

The next day Dad (John Mauldin) and I boarded a plane for a business trip and the dream flowed out in a waterfall of ideas as we refined it (as all good ideas on planes do). I knew this would become a book series. This was the strongest impression the dream had left me. As he'd done with other ideas I'd shared over the years, Dad told me to go for it. At the end of 2007 we started to interview our millionaires. The book was to be published the following year.

Well, life happened. I had one of the loves of my life, a little girl. I took other ideas from the back of a napkin he gave me and brought them to fruition, all the while never taking the folders far from my line of sight.

In 2015, I thought, "Why not see where our millionaires are today, after the Great Recession?" We reached out to them, and another round of interviews and research began.

Yet again, life brought a curve in the road.

Through all the gaps between the interviews, this book has always been just behind me, whispering ideas. I revisited their interviews, made countless notes on my phone or notepad (I still have quite a few of these, spanning years), and avidly researched the books and articles of this segment of the population. In March 2020, my father and I were walking along the beach and trail back to his home in Puerto Rico. I told him I wanted to reach out to our millionaires a third time. I could just feel this was it. He graciously said that he could see I was still passionate about it, and to go for it.

This set of interviews was like catching up with old friends. We genuinely were excited about their personal and business growth, and we were honored when they shared with us some not-so-easy moments.

There are so many more interviews that I hope to continue to share. There is a plethora of data and charts and statistical findings that would not fit in this book; hopefully, in the next.

Not everyone has shared my vision, but there is nothing else to say but that I have been compelled to bring this out into the world, to share a little bit of my life and the stories and lives of others. The connection between us is what it is all really about anyway.

While I cannot recall today the dream itself, the residue of the experience has followed me for 16 years. As you read these words, you have become a part of the magic of that dream.

ACKNOWLEDGMENTS

From John:
First and foremost, this book would have not been possible without Tiffani. It was her idea to start with. We started this project together in 2007, gathering data and doing hours and hours of interviews, but by the time we were ready it was already the Great Recession. Not a good time for publishing a book on millionaires. Seven years later, at her urging, we began to do a second round of interviews. Time passed. But she never lost her passion for the project, the people and their stories. And she once again picked up the gauntlet, we did a third round of interviews and while I participated, she has done the bulk of the work to bring this book to reality. Both the work of writing and editing – and the harder part of getting Dad to focus and keep up with her. She has been through storms, but she has brought this book into the harbor. I am proud of her and to be part of this project with her.

Second, I have to thank those who so willingly told their stories and went through multiple interviews. Who filled out loooong surveys and shared their lives with us.

Finally, I am grateful to my readers who allow me to come into their lives and give me the most precious thing of all – their time and attention. They make my life possible and I am humbly grateful.

From Tiffani:
There is no way that I could "acknowledge" a portion of all who have been a part of this creation the last 16 years. But I am gonna give it a go.

To you, dear reader. I have had this beating in my heart all this time … to share with you.

To our millionaires. So many of you didn't make this first book, and I hope to still share your stories. I really developed such a fondness for you all, your personalities, your passion, your frankness and struggles, and moments of vulnerability. You honor me with your stories, and I in turn honor you.

To my girls, Jessica, Ten, and Holls, for such real authentic support, the kind of friendship a woman really needs. To GLB (and Trish) who supported and followed my progress, or lack thereof sometimes, and always believed in the highest. To Ash, for getting goose bumps with me at "adult summer camp" when I decided to pick it back up again. To dear, dear Terra for being a witness and rare window to the evidence of that which is greater than us and a compass directing me to stoke that same light in me – and always answering my "can you read this edit please" texts.

A thank-you to Tyler Moore for your first dive into our data, and to Jamil for your extreme patience in this project and willingness to help wherever needed. Doug Harrison for countless times I needed access to the data … again. And Tammi "the right hand" Cole, for all you do and make happen for us!

To my slew of transcribers and personal editors and organizers from eons ago: Charley Sweet, Sommer "Dooley," Lynn Frederick, and Jeri Benjamin, and more.

I know I am forgetting someone. Oh yeah! Destiny Benjamin-Vandeput;). You have been there since day one with inspiration, transcripts, edits up to the end, random phone calls in my search for old documents, and help with heading titles – and with all my personal drama in between. Your love, support, and trust are priceless. And I'd better make the acknowledgments in your book.

To the team at Wiley, all the editors and behind-the-scenes work that completed this.

To Miss Vivace for your passion to be who you are and teaching me the same every day, and your patience for Momma needing early bedtimes for early writing mornings. Never stop the hugs!

And to my Daddy. None of this would be on paper if it wasn't for the legacy you have paved. The respect and love I have for your integrity, support, and example know no bounds. (Even if I had to re-pitch this to you a million times over the years.) I love you.

INTRODUCTION

A note from John:

Part of the theme in our findings is that there isn't a pattern. There are a lot of paths to achieving financial success, with as many different twists and turns on the way there. These stories have some major distinctions, but also themes of similarities.

Sometimes people think they have to do it through investing, in one way or another. But our research and the research of others indicate that's not always true. There are numerous ways to achieve financial independence. Very typically, that path is founding a business, making it grow, and adding value. It could also be an inheritance or taking your money and saving it, not living beyond your means – so that you do have money to save and invest.

We want to be able to show people what some of the roads taken are and to encourage people that, yes, you can do it.

This book is really about stories. I invite you to *eavesdrop on* these stories that illustrate all the unique plot twists on those paths. And then we add in some of the wisdom that we picked up on along the way.

We can't give you the "portrait of a millionaire" because, simply, our findings are all different ...

... so find what connects you.

A note from Tiffani:

I have grown quite fond of our millionaires. When you read thousands of words of transcripts and spend countless hours on each person's story, it's hard not to. There were moments of humor, many off-the-record discussions, too many tangents to mention, and a beautiful amount of vulnerability. We had to whittle all of that down to a couple of thousand words for each.

What is special about this book is that these aren't just ideas we compiled, sorted, and calculated on how to achieve financial success (though we do have data too). These are actual longitudinal case stories, if you will, of real-life experiences. They show how having certain characteristics, values, and mindsets works together over time.

> "Neuroeconomist Paul Zak has found that hearing a story with a narrative with a beginning, middle and end causes our brains to release cortisol and oxytocin these chemicals trigger the uniquely human ability to connect, empathize, and make meaning."
> —B. Brown, *Rising Strong*, 2015

When you read their story and connect with even one portion – it could be about their children and money, their upbringing that led them to an inspiration or business, a creative solution, or a mistake and how they learned from it – take note.

Try not to absorb just as a reader, but to experience what they did. Their background and life journey are provided to help you see through their eyes, to take a deep look at how their choices came about. Maybe it will come to mind when a choice develops in your own life. I am asking you to follow a fleeting inspiration, to connect and discover parts of yourself – because maybe you don't know what you want, desire, or which direction to go because it hasn't crossed your path yet (i.e., it doesn't exist yet).

Apply any "aha" moments into your own situation. Play freely with this script. This is a movie you are creating. Sense what it feels like with different choices you might make, inspired by the stories here.

Then take a breath. What will you do differently knowing what you know now? What could you incorporate from that insight into your life? Will cognitive dissonance play a part as you process these stories? Will you use a story to rationalize their behavior or your behavior, or will you accept reality and adjust?

Don't lose the thought – write it down.

I borrow from Malcolm Gladwell, as he says it best:

> "Good writing does not succeed or fail on the strength of its ability to persuade ... not this book anyway ... it succeeds or fails on strength of its ability to engage you, to make you think, to give you a glimpse into someone else's head – even if you conclude that someone else's head is not a place you'd really like to be."
> —Malcolm Gladwell, *What the Dog Saw and Other Adventures*, 2010

I consider this book a success if even one person is moved by an inspiring thought they can implement that brings them a deeper awareness and clearer direction in their own self and life.

From John and Tiffani:

I'm sure you will see our own fumbling in the rounds of interviews and the familiarity as we each grew as an interviewer and a person. Bear with us at the start, when we were going for facts in the first six years and then moved into what they had learned about life – it became about each person, what they experienced, and what that can mean to others.

Sometimes the facts repeat themselves in interviews that are 6 or 12 years apart. That is by design. If you hadn't talked to someone in 6 years and they asked you about something pivotal in your life, you might repeat yourself too. Some of the repetition we left, because it emphasized the importance of it to them, and it was said in a different way.

There are many, many more interviews and stories – including women, couples and international, pages of more data and charts, millionaires' Myers-Briggs personality test results (spoiler: our millionaires' results don't fall in the same personality distribution as the general population). Our hope is to release these and compile the conclusions and their patterns in the next book.

Finally, there is longevity in these stories. They may span the Great Recession, a bull market, and the pandemic, but the lifestyles, advice, financial implications, and decisions are timeless.

How to Read This Book

There are quite a few "millionaire" books out there. They each have their theme and more detailed advice to "that one way." But to echo John, what we have found is there is just simply *not* one way to financial freedom. This book is about those different ways.

Perhaps you connect with the story of saving and never having debt – so you combine it with a budgeting book.

Perhaps your heart rate sped up when you read the story about real estate – there is book for that too.

Perhaps – as many of our millionaires did – you follow your gut and instinct to not be in a 9-to-5 – or you have a need to be near mountains – so you follow that and the opportunities fall into place. Maybe you pick up *Secrets of the Millionaire Mind* next.

Perhaps you're inspired by the story of simply saving until a financial goal is reached, so *Automatic Millionaire* may be more up your alley.

Perhaps you find an innovative product and have an idea where there is a gap in the market, so you hunker down, knowing it will take a few years. You build that business by putting any money back into it and, barely take a paycheck – then sell it for a windfall – yes, there is a book for that, too.

Maybe you highlight some of the life lessons learned and mistakes made – and then formulate a personal map of your values to start choosing opportunities based on those hard-won lessons and the perceived failures of others.

If you buy this electronically – highlight your standouts and then take a moment to review other reader's highlights on your e-reader; or share with us on X (formerly Twitter), @Eavesdrop_On; Instagram, @EavesdroppingOn; or tag us on your social platform with #EavesdroppingOnMillionaires. If you like, follow us, and maybe something that didn't stand out to you in a story when you first read it will really hit home as a separate quote underlined or posted by someone else.

Pause and think for a few minutes about why you just highlighted a sentence – what that would mean to you.

There are so many insights and stories we did not have the space to share in this book. We wanted to continue to share their journeys they so generously offered. As we continue our research, we are sending out a millionaire story or topical insights every so often. This is completely free; we are just compelled to honor the others and share their equally inspiring stories. Just sign up at https://www.eavesdroppingon.com.

We use some icons over and over to emphasize a theme:

 · When you see this look for key insight, theme, or pivotal moment.

 This points to all things "numbers." It includes income, savings, spending, investments, business sales, change in net worth, and more.

 Often there is a piece of wisdom or a beautiful turn of phrase that merits a moment to pause and think. You will see this icon in the margin near those quotes.

Questions from Our Other Millionaires: When we started our third round of interviews, some of our millionaires began asking us questions. They were curious to hear the answers of the other people who were being interviewed. They let us know that they wanted to know what their peers were doing. This separate box at the close of each story are the answers to questions specifically posed by other millionaires.

Breakout Pages: As only 10 of our millionaires' complete stories made it into this book, that means we have stories and insights from hundreds of others. On these pages we organize some of their insights by specific topics.

Quotes to Ruminate On: These pages are also organized by topic – but just a sentence or two of concise answers to questions we posed to all our millionaires.

Chart Data: Our initial survey in 2008 and the follow up survey in 2023 produced over 23,000 unique surveys. We had over 100 questions and, but a few of these make up the charts in this book. We are excited to release more of the data in the future.

Insight Journal

Create Your Own Story: What do you love to do? What have you done that has been the most satisfying? What activities have always been easy for you that may be difficult for others? What do most people compliment you on? What was your best "mistake"? What would you do differently knowing what you know now? If you connected with something, put yourself in that situation, think about what you would have done or not done, and follow that imaginary path. If something gave you a bad taste in your mouth, consider why and what choices you would make differently.

Look back at what stood out to you, what you highlighted.

What were your "aha" moments? Don't lose the inspiration. Write it down now.

Our hope is that you find these stories as fascinating as we did, learning from the success of others, and find a few inspirational thoughts that you can translate into your own life. Now, let's eavesdrop on a few new friends …

CHAPTER 1

Rediscovering Purpose

A Hike, a Moment of Clarity, and Walking Away When It Doesn't Feel Fun

MEL A.
Net Worth: $18–20 Million
Income: $250K
Started Investing: 30
Attained Millionaire Status: 40

Quite a few of our millionaires had the trickle-down influence of parents who grew up during the Great Depression, and Mel is no exception. He grew up hearing stories about his grandfather, his namesake, and an entrepreneur. The man who led the family from their Iowa farm and then worked to build several businesses. The same man who lost most of it during the Depression. Mel describes looking up to him. "I remember him being kind of out there, willing to try anything and look after people."

When Mel was young, his father lost 90% of his eyesight, but still managed to maintain his income tax business. He remembers his father bent over, holding a piece of paper six inches away, viewing with a magnifying glass, always working tirelessly and never complaining. That was just what you did back then.

It was an era of not having much, and saving what you did have. There was no debt, and he cannot remember family fights about money.

Since Mel's blind father was eventually unable to fully support the family, his mom went back to work and took over management of their small real estate holdings.

"We never lacked, but we never had much. I remember we went out twice a month for dinner. That was a big thing in high school. If we even got pizza for takeout, that was an activity. There was camping, everyone loved the outdoors. My Mom would just let us explore and backpack while she was in a tent or little hotel building nearby.

"I had my first horse when I was 10. An Arabian Palomino named Abner. He was too much horse for a 10-year-old, but still could be amazingly gentle with a kid. I took care of him by myself for five whole years. I really enjoyed that and, you know, 'responsibility.' That was a significant part of my youth. Back then, I could get on the horse and ride through the hills all the way to Oakland. I could be gone all day as a 12-year-old kid and no one thought twice. Those days were good. I just really never thought about us having less money or lacking."

When Mel was younger, he got mediocre grades in school, but there was one teacher who saw his potential and put him in an advanced class.

He was convinced he was going to be the "dummy of the class," but his mom wouldn't let him give up. Her encouragement challenged him to dig in and study. This had the effect of ingraining in him that, despite what he was convinced of, he actually *could* do it. He went on to make good grades in high school and developed an interest in engineering. "It was the 1960s; we all saw a man on the moon and a lot of focus was on engineering, math, and sciences, so that was the direction I leaned." After graduating high school, he was accepted into UC Berkeley to study engineering.

It was the tail end of the Free Speech Movement in 1964 and 1965 and the beginning of the Vietnam War protests. Berkeley had long been a hotbed of radical thinking. In his first year at Berkeley, Mel was tear-gassed by riot police, and he remembers you could buy heroin on the corner if you wanted.

His wife's mother didn't allow her to go to Berkeley because of all this happening. In contrast, his mother had attended Berkeley in the 1930s – the time of people literally standing on soapboxes, communists professing dogma and theory. "Because of that, me going off to Berkeley in '68 didn't faze her at all," he said with a chuckle.

That first year he took a job at Edwards Air Force Base as part of a work/study program with the engineering school. "While I liked engineering, I looked at these guys that had been doing it for 10–15 years and they looked, well, kind of bored and locked in. They didn't go anywhere, just to some family commitments, and that kind of spooked me. Being an engineering major, I realized that was all I would focus on, and I had always wanted to take some English and maybe go to law school. That spook had me ending up transferring to a major in business as the prep for law school and I did actually minor in English Literature."

He only pursued the minor because he wanted to broaden his exposure and improve his writing. He is the first to admit that he was taking classes with English majors who were clearly much better at it than him. "I was just happy to be there, and if I ever got a B, I was typically happy."

While in college, Mel led mountaineering trips in the summer. He would take people out for 2–3 weeks at a time to experience nature, which also seated in him a respectful orientation to the environment. He looks back at those trips as one of the most formative times of his life, teaching him the joy of doing something he was really good at.

He interviewed for jobs in his last two years of college and realized, yet again, he couldn't see himself working a nine-to-five job. So, of course, he decided to do what he was good at and lead more trips. That winter he lived on the Southside of Chicago. "At that time, I had the smallest apartment. I'll always remember that you could open up the sofa bed and it touched the wall on the other side, but I wasn't there a lot, so that worked fine for me."

One September, when all the camps had finally closed and all the kids had gone home, he decided to take one more hiking trip. "I still remember it was a distinct experience and realization. I came back and asked myself 'Why am I doing this?' I had already hiked 1,000 miles that summer. I didn't *need* to hike another 30. I realized the reason I liked doing it was working with people and being with groups of young kids. That is what gave it a purpose. That realization made me start thinking what else I wanted to do in life."

A friend suggested business school to explore more directions. "Maybe it wasn't an immediate answer to what I wanted to do, but it was a good way to do something that would lead to another step. I remembered that I had taken a real estate class years before; there had been a case study on a project in New York and the professor asked, 'Who would like to do this?' I kind of snuck my hand up. What I had liked about that project was that it was a combination of designing.

It combined engineering, quantitative math, some architecture and legal activity which appealed to my interest in law.

"That moment had stuck in my mind. I called up that same real estate professor and told him what I was thinking. He suggested three or four business schools. So, when I went to business school, it wasn't so I could get a job that would make me a lot of money; it was just following what I liked to do."

Mel's college tuition for one quarter was $150 and another $150 for room and board. His mother had some real estate that she had inherited that helped cover some of that. In business school, that real estate was able to fund the tuition portion, and he got a job to pay for his room and board.

While he was at Wharton School at Pennsylvania University, he took a job at a Fortune 500 company that owned trucking and shipping companies. They were building LNG tank carriers from the aftermath of the high oil prices in the early 1970s and the oil embargo. He worked in the fairly small corporate planning department.

"It ended up being quite interesting. The guy I worked for had been a professor at a PhD program for economics. He was like having a private tutor for the next year." It was through this relationship that he discovered what he truly wanted to do. He decided to pursue his interest in real estate, specifically development activity. He connected the dots from his earlier thought in life that he might love the development and project management side of business.

His love of having topography around him, wanting mountains at the door, pushed him to look west. He found a position back in Los Angeles to do corporate banking for real estate lending and the energy sector.

During this time in business school, Mel met his wife, who was in the same business training program through UCLA. "We are grateful that our children grew up when we didn't have a lot," Mel reflects. "My wife clipped coupons, and we went camping for vacations. What we realize *now* is that if you work hard enough, are effective enough, and take those chances when they come up, you can succeed," he says, echoing his Mom's encouragement from childhood.

He went to work in corporate banking, handling construction lending to small companies regionally. He soon realized they were lending 90% of the monies these construction companies needed in order to build, *but* they were only getting paid "prime plus a kiss."

"We thought, why don't we lend a little bit more and get a piece of the equity transaction?" He got approval and began allocating $100 million to go into industrial buildings and then into residential buildings. He built up a small team to do profit participation loans. They went through the first $100 million in nine months and felt they were on a pretty good track, got approval for another round, and continued that course, growing his team to 25 people.

This was at a time when real estate in California was extremely lucrative. "That was pretty much the crux of our activity, and it grew until we had done about $2 billion in lending activities." Then the recession of the 1990s was upon him, and they wound down that activity. He utilized the range of experience he had gathered in developing in a move to be responsible for the REO (real estate owned) activity.

Like many of our millionaires, Mel had the instinct to leave his job when it stopped being fun. "I could have stayed on, but I was offered a package that let me walk away with three years of income, so that's exactly what I did. I left the comfort of the big company that never paid huge amounts, but was comfortable, and I got a decent bonus. The job had been safe, I guess, but it was not something I wanted to do anymore." He considers his "best mistake" to be leaving the corporate world.

When he left the banking industry, he was worth $1 million, had debt of $600,000 from remodeling his house, so was liquid only $250,000.

At that time, he and his wife *still* didn't have a long-term savings plan. They maxed out their IRAs every year but didn't save much above that.

Mel decided to take out $150,000 of what he had to start a small business.

He ended up losing it entirely. Every penny. A friend was doing specialty marketing manufacturing and had some ideas for licenses to a big company for limited edition watches. He wanted some help and Mel signed up with his $150,000.

Off to China they went. "In that whole experience, while unprofitable and not successful for a variety of reasons, the key lesson learned was that the quality of the product and the idea doesn't make any difference if you can't get what I would call 'distribution' – if you can't get the product in front of people.

"It was an eye-opening experience into how things worked. I came away realizing if you wanted to make anything and do it in mass production, not necessarily the highest quality, you had better want 10,000 of them. This was due to the manufacturing setup and the assembly line to crank them out was not worth it below that number to the manufacturers. The whole experience itself was worth the money I had invested, which was a lot at that time.

"Now, for a number of years I regretted that, but in hindsight it gave me a different perspective from people in the corporate world. It taught me to be entrepreneurial, to be solely dependent on what I could do for myself. That attitude helped me greatly when I went out and started my own investment management business."

Let us remind you that Mel hadn't been paid during that year and a half venture, where he also lost his shirt. The women in his life came to the rescue. Mel's mom once again stepped in and covered about 70% of their mortgage payment, and Mel's wife was able to cover the day-to-day expenses, food, and utilities. They didn't spend much and vacations were camping trips, just like when he was a kid. "We just kind of got by and always seemed to have enough for the next thing down the road."

Through his previous relationship with the employer he considered a mentor; it came full circle, and he was asked to join a new venture. It was the right time in the market, as CalPERS (California Public Employees' Retirement System) had initiated a real estate investment program in previous years and they were looking to expand by adding a land development program where they felt there was a need for capital support in California.

This had been primarily done through the savings and loans through the 1980s, and now those S&Ls were gone and couldn't provide that. They ultimately got approved by CalPERS for a large equity capital allocation. Then relationships with other entities formed and so they started their own capital firm.

The first year, he and his partner couldn't pay themselves, yet again. "We each contributed $5,000 to the company to pay our secretary and cover the next three months. We figured if we could get through the first year, we'd make some money. We got paid in fees, we basically got an origination fee and spread that over the life of the project. In hindsight, it was pretty attractive. We would leave the excess profits in there to run the business. The origination and management fees and the profit incentive fees were what we would take out. And we just kept doing that.

"We were trying to hit singles; we weren't trying to hit a home run or take any big risks. We were trying to do solid deals. I remember when we would do a typical home building transaction, we would get $300,000 of the origination fees, and if it did well, we might get a projected $300,000 of incentive fees. I was like, this is a lot of money for two guys who were just kind of scrapping things together."

From that business that was just trying to hit singles, Mel ended up making about $40 million. After paying $18 million in taxes, he had approximately $22 million take-home. "I probably got a little carried away at the racetrack, as I was doing a little racing on the side, and I lost some of that money on that … a bit foolish."

He invested a large chunk of his money but currently still has $10 million in cash and owns his house outright, and also a second home they bought with the profits. He also has about $2 million in stocks. Even with a net worth of $18–20 million, he and his family live on $150,000 a year (after taxes) and are comfortable with that. "That salary won't let me do some of the things I would like to do, but it's adequate. Occasionally, I'll take out profits to do something unusual, like a trip to Africa.

"I am conscious of protecting what I have. I will probably always keep 20–30% in relatively liquid investments. I am deciding on how much to direct myself. I found I love doing real estate investments – rolling up my sleeves and getting into them. I don't have the same satisfaction of studying companies and looking for value. It is just not as much fun. To the extent that I can have an investment advisor that will direct some of that side, it is useful."

His kids grew up in the early years before he made most of his money, and because of that they are very grounded and not materialistic. Like their father, his kids are well read and like to think about things. "I have raised them to make their own decisions. Instead of working for a ski shop, how about owning your own ski shop, son?"

Mel said he could retire if he wanted too, but he doesn't. "I mean, if I retire, I would probably go find something else to do. I like real estate. I have a lot to offer people."

Mel never lost the love for the outdoors he developed leading treks in his younger years. He enjoys skiing, snowshoeing, and hiking, as they provide him tremendous peace of mind and tranquility. He also reads 60-plus hours a week – titles ranging from nonfiction to biographies on Lincoln and other presidents. "I read this interesting book called *God and Gold* studying how Anglo-Saxon cultures in particular did better economically versus France and Italy. It struck me as interesting. I remember in the Berkeley bookstore I was in the economics section, and I picked up this 700-page book. It was about tracking economics and military advancement over the last 500 years, analyzing why some cultures did better than others. It was fascinating, but I have also read all the Harry Potter books too," he said with a laugh.

When asked why he focuses so much on nature and literature, he quotes Laurance Rockefeller: "In the midst of the complexities of modern life, with all its pressures, the spirit of a man needs to refresh itself by communion with unspoiled nature. In such surroundings – occasional as our visits may be – we can achieve that kind of physical and spiritual renewal that comes alone from the wonder of the natural world."

Mel is proud of what he's accomplished so far. "If I could pass down something to future generations, it would be that we don't control most things in life, but we can control our own consciousness. We can control how we let outside events impact our thinking and mental equilibrium. Knowing this, we have a great deal of control over our own happiness and mental well-being."

SIX YEARS LATER ...
Net Worth Increased to $23 Million

JOHN: Let's talk about where you've been. You are 64 now; give us an update on the last few years.

MEL: Well to start, we had a real estate investment company that, unfortunately, we haven't done a lot of new business in.

It was definitely in a market that was headed down. We got our investors a 20% return on their money. It wasn't 30%, but 20% was pretty good, and they got all their money back.

I looked at a variety of opportunities in the downturn. They were mostly in real estate. I had a couple of properties in escrow that didn't close because they were too speculative. They were quality properties with very low cap rates.

I also own a shopping center with some family. I looked at selling it, but I can't find anything I would rather buy. I am more retired than I was.

I am looking at buying an interest in a boutique hotel that would be a longer-term family business with my two sons. I need to make sure I am not doing it for emotional reasons, though. I realize people buy hotels sometimes for emotional reasons. I want to make sure it is a reasonable investment. The idea of having a cash-flow-producing, operating business has an appeal to it, as opposed to more passive investments. There are some new developments where we could expand it from 40–60 rooms and upgrade it. It is something that spurred my interest a long-time ago.

TIFFANI: Let's go into that, because I have a quote from you where you wanted your kids to make their own decisions. "Instead of working for a ski shop, how about owning your own ski shop?" You are going with them into a hotel? How have they turned out?

MEL: Years ago, we took a family vacation and stayed at this hilltop hotel in Tuscany that a businessman from Milan had bought and fixed up. He was semi-retired, and he just did it because he wanted to do something to keep his income up. I looked at that and thought it was interesting. It was a nice way to meet people, as you can kind of visit with them. I am basically a shy person, but if I had a reason to talk with someone, I could go talk to anyone. So that is what piqued my interest. I always liked the mountains, and I liked skiing, so that got me focused on location.

I started taking some classes at Cornell and my wife said, "Make sure you are doing this for yourself, and don't saddle your sons with something that they don't have any interest in." So, I went down the road of looking at my own motivations. I wanted the hotel to be something that was in my own interest. If they wanted to come along at some point and get involved, if they were qualified and had the right education and training, then they could do that.

The boys have actually been working at ski resorts. One has been on ski patrol at a place for a number of years. Neither planned to do it this long, but once they started it was hard to leave, so they have continued. They have both worked in restaurant businesses in both resort environments and in Boulder. Both went to school there, and one spent his summers there.

TIFFANI: Is your point in doing that hotel to have your kids be more financially independent versus being at a ski resort? Or is it just something to do for family reasons?

MEL: They did think about owning a restaurant and doing it together. That was not with any of my involvement, but they probably realized dad would pitch in and help if they could do a good job at it. So, I really started the hotel without their involvement.

I would love to see them have a business and be more independent. I would rather see them owning a business and not just getting paid day to day. I think they have matured, and they are both really interested in that. So, I started negotiating some things and doing some due diligence. I asked if the boys wanted to come along, and they did.

I have gotten a lot of pleasure out of that, as this is the first time I've ever done anything business-wise with them. I have appreciated their insights and thoughts and input. I value that, and it's a lot more fun to do something with people you enjoy working with than to do it on your own. Given that they are family, and we have a really good relationship, I certainly get gratification out of doing something with them.

TIFFANI: I personally understand the fulfillment that comes with that. When we first interviewed you, you said your net worth was $18–20 million and your income was about $150,000. What do you think it is today?

MEL: I would say the net worth is probably a little higher. Some of the real estate assets have gone down, but my securities have gone up. I have some real estate that I have kind of written off in my mind that could potentially have a windfall to it. I have taken those write-downs in my mind since 2007. Real estate went down about $5 million, but stocks probably went up by something similar.

TIFFANI: That was another thing I was going to ask you. You said you were keeping 20–30% liquidity. Is that something you still do?

MEL: I probably have $9–10 million in a variety of liquid things. From private debt to a bond portfolio to stocks. I probably have $10–12 million in real estate. That doesn't count my family real estate. Probably $8 million in homes and another $6 million in shopping centers.

JOHN: Were you worried during the last six years, after the 2008 crisis?

MEL: Oh yes. I was under contract to buy a high-end piece of real estate in Hawaii. I walked away from a $75,000 deposit because I didn't want to close on it. That was probably the best decision I made, despite the $75,000 loss, as the project ended up going bankrupt. That would have been worse, because I would have owned a condo in a bankrupt project. In the two years after our interview, we canceled some trips. We were going to Antarctica, and we canceled that. We kind of hunkered down. Then I saw what happened in the residential land business. In California it had just gotten way overpriced, which I had known in 2008, and it just crumbled. People are always looking for deals and I saw some people buy some things as the market came down and they still paid too much because the market kept going down. We used to have over a million housing permits a year and we are not even remotely close to that. We have an aging house stock, and at some point, you have to think of replacement housing too.

TIFFANI: What has your income been like?

MEL: I don't like spending principal. I have had enough income – from dividends and income and particularly my family property – that I don't think about income much. The family property happens to be doing really well. It generates a decent cash flow. That is why I looked at maybe selling it, but by the time I paid taxes and redeployed it and thought of the loss of that cash flow … it is just easier to keep it.

TIFFANI: You are taking your dividends and income off the top, but not touching principal. Why are you saving your principal?

MEL: It was just the function of how I was raised. You just never spend your principal.

TIFFANI: That is quite a lot of principal. Are you waiting to pass it down? You are old enough now where you could start using it.

MEL: Yes, it is. We kind of live a lifestyle, and it is a comfortable lifestyle. We are leaving for Austria to look at Austrian hotels and then we are doing a walking trip through southern Italy. We have done biking trips all over: Normandy, Czech Republic, Vienna. We have been traveling more. If that happens to take in a little principal, that doesn't bother me. I have a couple of sport cars I race. I just bought a 1935 Bentley so I can do longer cross-country rallies. That is a couple hundred thousand dollars. You could think of it as consumption, but I view it as an asset. I took money out of my stock account to do that.

TIFFANI: How are you protecting that money? Do you have a trust?

MEL: I basically have everything in a family trust. Most people should unless they are going to generate some liabilities. A trust helps from a tax standpoint. It is only if you are out there, particularly on the real estate side, where you get into personal guarantees or partnerships you are involved with that people have liabilities they haven't thought of. That would be the only excuse for people not to get a trust.

TIFFANI: So, regardless of the fact that you are retired, you told us before that you would have to still find something to do, and you now have the hotel project. Your wife is keeping busy even though technically she is retired. Both of you – retired or not – are making sure you are doing stuff.

MEL: I am sometimes not as busy as I would like to be. In the last six years, there were probably transition periods where I felt like I wasn't being productive and doing things. It was one of the things about the hotel and why I decided to pursue it – it would help keep me busy. It gives me an outlet of activity, and it's something I could be occupied with and still have someone to professionally help run it, and I could be as involved as I want.

TIFFANI: Can you give us one more story from Berkeley? You remember tear gas and heroin on the corner; do you remember another story from that time that has stayed with you?

MEL: There is one event that sticks in my mind. I started in 1968, and they had an event they called People's Park. It got national news, and it was a pretty silly thing in hindsight. The university owned a vacant lot near campus, and local people – not students but more of the hangers-on, as I would call them – had started growing things there. The university decided they wanted to put a building on it, and there were these riots to protect People's Park. They tried to find solutions, and ultimately the University gave up. Five years later, some young people that I happened to be standing with said there was a riot to mark the anniversary of People's Park, and they wanted to go watch. It struck me that it had become entertainment. I still have this vivid vision of this guy, might have been 18 or 19, walking down the street. He had a rock in his hand and he was smashing the glass on parking meters. He was blocks away from the activity, as if this was his contribution to the riot. I was just shaking my head. Their involvement was an act of frustration and had nothing to do with the issues around the event itself. That was an odd thing that stuck out that I still remember.

TIFFANI: I would love to have just an interview about that time. All right, obviously you are still hiking. You told us before that the mountaineering and everything you did to train for it has influenced you and still comes through in your life. Can you still connect that love now to what you experienced back then?

MEL: Not necessarily. Both my wife and I are passionate about the outdoors. We just enjoy being in the mountains. Particularly, there is something about the alpine region, taking in the view above the tree line. Whether it be summer, winter, or fall, we go snowshoeing in the winter, and ski and hike. We raised our kids in that environment, which is probably why they do what they do because they just like being there. Yes, I was introduced to it when I was young, but it was embedded into our family because we all enjoy doing it.

I am typically very active. I recently did a 280-mile, 34-day hike. I did it with a friend. Some people do it faster, but I just did it because I wanted to be out there for a long time. We carried tents, 50-pound packs, and a week's supply of food.

Another time, we were in Colorado, near Aspen, visiting friends who have a second home there. We took a hike and got up above the tree line. I was ahead of the rest of the group and stopped and was sitting by a little stream that was coming down through the short alpine grasses. My wife came up, and I said, "Welcome home." To me, up there has always felt like another sort of home. That is why I do it, whether it's summer or winter. It's very personally satisfying.

TIFFANI: What within yourself do you attribute to your financial and business success?

MEL: Integrity. I always tried to treat people the way I would want to be treated. As a result, people wanted to do business with me.

Most important life lesson
Doing what you say you are going to do. Work hard and you will be all right. You will always have what you need.

What do you see as the next big thing?
Alternative energy and biotech

(continued)

Luxury items worth the money
A second home in the mountains, and I do enjoy my Porsche on a winding road. I have two, one 2001 and one 1973. I race vintage sports cars as a hobby.

Favorite books
Harry Potter; *Lord of the Rings*; westerns (all the Louis L'Amour books); *Bourne Identity* books; books that explore why things in history developed economically and socially the way they did; the *Bible*.

SIX *MORE* YEARS LATER ...
Net Worth Increased

Mel was the first interview we continued with, six years later, 12 years after our first meeting. What you can't read on the page is the smiles on our faces, and just how happy we were to be starting again and catching up.

We had so many questions. At the top of our list was the boutique hotel. Did it work out as a business? Were his sons now involved?

"This hotel was actually quite significant. I had started taking classes at Cornell, in their hospitality school, so I could be more educated about the industry. We did not do anything at that time with that hotel, as the seller was not someone we decided we wanted to partner with. He was going to be unreasonable. He had his own way of how he wanted to do things and, and so forth.

"First, let me tell you about the experience with my son who had gone to the University of Colorado. He started ski patrol and thought he would do that for just a few years. He ended up doing it for 10 years and, you know, life was pretty good when he could get up and get fresh powder and throw dynamite and start avalanches. But he realized he needed to do something else at some point.

"That experience made him realize that he didn't have the business background he would need to go do something else. He ended up going back and getting an MBA at Colorado with the sole intent of coming back to Mammoth and working for the mountain resort.

"He never interviewed with a company at school through all their interview programs. He came back a second year in the winter. Then he had a moment with the president of the mountain. The guy liked him a lot. Liked the idea that, you know, you could bring in professionally trained people to work in a process to change the old school culture of 'doing things the way they always did them.' He went from ticket sales to dealing with customers that were frustrated, so many stories. He has moved to hill safety and he is in the main office now. He enjoys doing that.

"Let me go back to the hotel, I had become friends with the manager of a boutique hotel and phoned them up. We hired my son for the summer, and the owner that we had thought he did a great job. So, he got a little bit of his hands in the hotel industry. We have not given up the opportunity. It may still come together.

"What I *did* do is invest in a boutique hotel in Palm Springs. This was partially to learn more about the business. I thought I could learn a lot from the manager. It was doing really well, 4-star rated, one of the best hotels in the area. Then they had to close. I had a very unique investment structure. I basically invested money and got a pledge. They had a deal with the city that they got a rebate of 50% of their hotel tax up to a certain dollar amount. I got a pledge of that money, so it protected my principal. So, I did take my hope of opening a boutique hotel interest a little further."

So, now for the numbers.

Mel had half of his net worth in real estate, another $6 million in shopping centers, 30% liquid and not living off the principal. Where are we now? And our burning question is where is that principal going to be distributed at the end of their lives?

Mel currently has half of his liquidity with an investment firm that is an "all in," long-only stock firm. He found the firm through a friend who had managed her parents' money well. The stocks shift in his portfolio in different industries depending on the cycles. The roller coaster pandemic market came along. He left it all in, and it came a bit back up. He has expectations that the market will still go down but is leaving it where it is.

"I am happy we own our own residence free and clear. I kind of view that whether the stocks go up or down, not a big deal for us. I do remind myself that there are 60% of people, or some number like that, that don't have emergency money over a few hundred dollars.

"I do own a lot more gold stocks; I started acquiring some five years ago. They didn't do much for a while. And remember, I am not a great trader of my own investments. Things I am interested in, the real estate industry and projects, I tend to buy stocks and just leave them alone. I remember two months ago looking at my gold portfolio and it was up 30% for the year. I was like, 'Well, that's good.' I did some research and decided to load up again, principally on mining stocks. I have this kind of a backstop, you know, if things get really strange out there.

"My family sold the shopping center and I put some of that in the hotel and some of it went to our travel budget. Philosophically, I still desire to not live off principal. If the market were dropping, well for now, I have never taken money out of the money. I never touched it even in the last crisis.

"We have the wills made out and a few tax-exempt entities that we support – a school and environmentally related organizations. We have carved out several million dollars that will go to a variety of charitable institutions. I certainly wouldn't leave it all to them. After that, most of it probably goes to our kids. Fifteen years ago, when we talked, the balance was substantially less than it is today. So, we have talked about if we are going to change that.

"In the back of my mind I have that desire to acquire that boutique hotel in Jackson Hole and own it, and leave it to my two sons to run."

What would happen if the market goes down another 30–40%? How does that affect the lifestyle of someone that has quite a lot of principal We asked, "Would anything really change with that kind of market drop, since you have the funds to continue the way you are currently living?" Not surprisingly, Mel had a different perspective.

"Now, it probably doesn't force us to change our lifestyle, but we would change, for two reasons. One, it just doesn't seem prudent to do some of the things that we did. We live pretty economically. Other than having two hobbies, we travel a fair amount, and we spend money on that. We would probably not anymore. It is too visible. I don't want to be out there doing that, if the world is struggling. You know, kind of living it up and not caring about what is happening to others.

"Second, there is the issue that you don't want to outspend your money - in terms of how long you are going to be around. We are both quite healthy. I am about to go on another weeklong backpacking trip with my kids.

"I'll tell you what, our travel is one of the more expensive topics. We do focused traveling with a company called Lindblad. They go to weird places and take different ships, like Antarctica. Those can cost $20,000 a piece."

Wait! Mel had postponed that trip over a decade ago during the financial crisis. Now they took that trip. They finally made it happen.

"It was a real wonderful trip. We would love, love to do it again. But, we did actually postpone another trip during *this* crisis. Our other travel thing is we do bicycle trips with a company called Butterfield & Robinson.

"The other hobby I still have is vintage cars. When we first talked, I had a few older Porsches. I got as fast as I was going to get with them. When you race, it is a lot of sitting around. You might get onto the track 3–4 times for 20 minutes of time. You are getting cars ready but sitting around more. I decided that I like doing rallies, you are just busy more and all day you are seeing things. I have a couple of cars in England, and I do rallies with them that can last a week or two. Last year, I did a rally that went through the old part of what was Yugoslavia and another rally that went from London to Spain. Then between trips, the Arctic twice, and we loaded up on a bicycle trip in Norway.

"Oslo has to be one of my favorite cities I have ever been to. I would go back there in a minute. It is walkable and friendly, urban but not too crowded. They have a wonderful park there with a local artist you can go see. We took a train from there to the western side of the mountains to Bergen. Then we did a private bike tour along the edge and stayed in little remote hotels. We would go kayaking one day and hiking the next. I would do that trip in a minute again. A bit more extravagant than a normal travel year."

Because I am sure you are wondering, we did ask. He spent about $100,000 that year on travel. Their yearly income is still the same but enjoying the fruits of their labor has come in the form of travel and vintage car experiences. The experiences are not just about the destination for Mel.

"It is a nice way to meet most of my socialization needs. When I worked, well I am not the most gregarious, outgoing person in groups. I am kind of one on one, but I had that at work. The trips, especially the vintage road rallies, I have a chance to meet lots of people. I see them from one event to the next, and it is not that we become close friends, but get to have interesting conversations. I would visit a few of them in England or Scotland if I was there. It has contributed to a more interesting life, you could say."

What we really enjoyed about these third interviews was the familiarity for us in catching up. We can't leave out Mel's voice lighting up when he talked about his sons or the beauty of where his home is, and in his excitement in sharing about travel.

If you are thinking about what you read in the previous interview – Mel discussed needing to stay busy, possibly not being busy enough, needing to keep finding a business for his time, but now he is traveling and seemingly living the traditional retired life – just wait.

"So, I bought a racetrack years ago. It was a terrible thing to do. I sunk a lot of money into it. We got shut down for environmental reasons; it was not a great business in itself and about three miles from San Francisco. We have managed to get it entitled and approved as a remote test facility. We have got at least two – one is an electric car maker that uses it as their test facility. I have kept busy pulling that together. I am dealing with entitlements, refurbishing old improvements that were there, providing our own fire system with storage tanks. Nothing overly complex, but it certainly has kept me busy. I have three or four things I am still involved in. I have an agreement with an American Indian tribe to help them get entitlements for a casino at some point, so that will be a portion of my time.

"Mammoth is one of the largest ski resorts in the country. It is on the Eastern side of the Sierras, which puts us in an unusual location. You really can only drive up from Southern California. It is a lovely drive, hardly any traffic. You don't get many people from the Bay Area here because the passes are mountain roads west, and they are closed in the winter time. They would have to drive by all the other resorts, like the Lake Tahoe area. So, they don't come here. We get better snow. We are about 2,000 feet higher; the base of the mountains is about 8,000 feet compared to those other resorts. It began as a fishing and mining town. Really it is not far from the Nevada line tax wise. If it *were* in Nevada, I'd probably make that my permanent residence, but I don't have that luxury.

"Our days here look like waking up and letting your eyes take in the mountains. Take a nice walk. We have had 10 feet of snow at times, and then it is 80 degrees outside. We enjoy the outdoors. There is definitely a different stress level from when we go back down to Los Angeles."

What stands out about Mel's journey is he worked long, pulled out of something more than once because he just didn't enjoy doing it. He had a number in his head, he hit it with his first big sell, and then kept the principal and lived the life he wanted to live. Mel politely corrected that statement.

"I never had a real number. But the number I hit was far bigger than I ever could have picked. I probably don't think of it as long and hard. I happened to choose something I really enjoyed doing. I was in the right place at the right time and happened to be good at what I did. We could successfully structure an investment fund, we got guys promoted out of it, we made other people money. And so, we made a lot of money for ourselves.

"You know, my wife clipped coupons for food. My kids still remember that once we had come back from a ski trip that had run up some credit card debt. We went into a restaurant, a national chain, and sat down and looked at the menu. I was just seeing, well you know, what the final bill was going to come in at. We literally got up and left the restaurant because the menu was too expensive. My kids still remember that, in a positive way.

"We enjoy some nice vacations, but other than that, in some ways, I feel we live the same. I am looking down at this wonderful hand-made walnut desk that was made in Wyoming for me. I am sitting in front of it, kind of western style. I would have bought that before the money. It is not extravagant. It is just a really nice handmade desk with a two-inch piece of walnut on the top. So, we have little pieces we have given ourselves. Life is wonderful. I would say the most important thing is family."

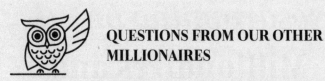

QUESTIONS FROM OUR OTHER MILLIONAIRES

What is important to you and how has that changed over time?
As much as I enjoyed what I did at work, we'd go to New York to raise money, talk to people. I used to have a joke about wearing my New York suit to go to Wall Street. I look back and I would have no interest in repeating that. We dealt with the nice people on Wall Street and you know, we always had a really good relationship with them. But it isn't as important as it used to seem. It is more now, how do you want to spend your time?

Our kids are busy, but we spend more time with family, kids, and our travels. We meet some pretty interesting people when we travel, and I've gotten to be really good friends with them.

It is the friendships and people that are more important than being busy.

eavesdropping on

Millionaires and Their Children

> "Here's what we say to our kids about being successful. One can get straight As and we are really darn happy if he gets a C and a couple of Bs. But quite frankly, they will both be successful in different ways because they have very different strengths. We tell them there are multiple ways to become successful. There is no guarantee of doing XYZ or going to the right school or doing this and that is going to take you there. It has to do with how you plot your path and it's all different ways. I think that message for my kids is important. I want them to know. I think sometimes these kids get out of school these days and they feel like they've gotten a degree and it's supposed to happen for them. But no. There are all different ways to get there and you have to find your way. "
>
> —Tracie

> "My kids earn an allowance every week, even the 3-year-old. He doesn't have to do much for it. Every Sunday I sit down with them and say, 'What did you do to help the family this week? Did you help clean up the communal space? Not just your regular chores you would do as young children, but what did you do extra and above? Did you tidy up the toy room, did you do this for Mom, that for Mom?' They each have to tell me what they did. It may be one thing, or it may be something every day, they are still very young. So they get $5 or $6 for allowance. The 3-year-old will get $3 and the 6- and 8-year-old each get $6. So I've tried to teach them. When

(continued)

it comes to presents, they buy the presents with their own money. If they really want a particular toy (obviously we buy them things) they go out and they open up the piggy bank and they go buy it themselves. When it comes to Christmas gifts and birthday gifts, they buy those for their brothers and sisters with their own money. So that's the idea that money has a value, but you have to earn it, number one, and number two, it's partly for you and it's partly for sharing your love with other people."

—Desmond

"We try to remind them constantly that what they have is not theirs and is not something they should feel entitled to, or that it makes them 'better,' because they haven't done anything to have it. Really it is trying to tone down any arrogance."

—Lowery

"You don't have to be the smartest and the brightest, but you've got to get up in the morning, you've got to go to work, and you've got to work hard. You can't be the worker who takes off Friday and skips Saturday to go on a trip. If you've got a job, you work hard and you get ahead. You don't have to be the best and the brightest to be really good at something and attract attention and get promoted. But you can't be a goof off. It worked for me, and I think it's worked for my kids."

—Al

CHAPTER 2

Slow and Steady Wins the Race

RICHARD K.
Net Worth: $1–1.5 Million
Income: $100–200K
Started Investing: 17
Attained Millionaire Status: 23

With dozens of interviews under our belt, we thought we had started to see a pattern that most wealth is accumulated after a windfall of money or a few big hits. It could be the sale of a business or piece of property, an inheritance, or an incredible dividend return from an investment or retirement package; just something that gave them a nest egg to begin their journey to wealth.

Richard, however, blew that theory out of the water when we learned about his savings discipline that paved his road to becoming a millionaire.

Richard grew up fascinated with the world around him. When he attended college, his intention was to become a botanist, but that wasn't enough; he decided to expand that to major in biochemistry, just so he could take a broader scope of classes. "Changing meant that I would take the widest range of courses, plus a lot of courses outside of the sciences. I didn't go to college for a career. I went to college for an education."

Even though he became a millionaire relatively early, he had a rough time in the early 1980s. "I got hit real hard in the recession. It was a lot of everything at once. I was kind of burnt out on what I was doing before." Instead of staying with it and pushing through, he followed an instinct that he just wasn't enjoying what he was doing.

He thought about one of his college courses that had stood out. It was not in the botany or biochemistry departments. It was psychology. That fascination for learning took over again. "I really just thought, 'Well, I will go back and get some education in that area.' I specialized in the alcohol and drug treatment area of that program."

With everything that he was doing and all the study that a PhD entails, he became immersed in the drug and alcohol treatment arena. Because of this focus, he happened to hear about a recent law passed requiring drug testing for truck drivers.

Like any good entrepreneur, Richard saw a need that was not being met and found the solution. "At that time, I was in the process of setting up for a doctoral program in psychology to sort of keep 'the lights on.' I thought, 'There is nobody providing services to trucking companies for this alcohol and drug program. I know the alcohol and drug field. I know how to work with these companies, so I'll start a business.'

"I learned the regulations and began to let it be known that I was available to those companies. There are a fair amount of agriculture and trucking companies near here. It is a fairly small community. I actually did a little bit of marketing in the beginning. It was sort of a waste of time, because it became just word of mouth after that. Then the business took off and it has been very successful. Science is still my first love. In fact, part of the reason I am semi-retired is to get back into the sciences and work in that area."

Richard was able to semi-retire after a search for someone to bring into his business. He was on the hunt for someone that was qualified to take on that specific kind of work. "It is very detail oriented; you have a lot of responsibility. It is sometimes a life-or-death situation. For a variety of reasons, it was hard to find somebody that was a good match. I finally did, and that person handles the day-to-day routine and freed up a lot of my time."

His own financial journey is a reflection of "slow and steady wins the race." Richard estimates his net worth to be around $1.5 million and has accumulated most of that through savings.

He saves approximately 85% of his $125,000 income every year. That is not a typo: 85%. His home, rental property, and car are paid off and although his expenses are low, the rising cost of healthcare is his biggest concern. "I think besides health insurance, I have expenses of maybe $15,000 a year. I share my house with someone that contributes. I buy food ... a little gas. The things I like to do don't cost a lot of money. I don't buy boats and planes or things like that."

Richard started investing while he was in college and got his feet wet during a time when the market was essentially flat. "I didn't like the bond market at that time because you couldn't really name your price. Your costs were hidden, and you couldn't go in and say. 'I want to sell this now.' Then I stumbled across the whole trust-preferred bonds and found what I was looking for."

After retiring, Richard moved most of his investment profile from equities to bond-type instruments. He likes this because even if bonds are down, they are still paying interest unless the company goes bust.

"I am not sweating like I would be in this market if I was still in equities and wondering if it would bounce back. If I do some homework, I can get an even 8%. I am figuring, OK, equities in the long run are supposed to give you 11%. I am giving up 3%, but I've cut my risk down far. Is it worth it to me to give up that 3% when I don't need that 3%? The answer was clearly, yes. The prices going down doesn't bother me tremendously because that isn't money that I depend on for a living."

His savings is divided between a 401(k), defined benefit plan, Roth IRA, and an HSA (Health Savings Account). They each always get fully funded, and he can put more money into the defined benefit plan. "I do spend a lot of time on the investments. I hope to keep it growing. Lately I have been buying like crazy, but I have used up all my cash. I can't put any more into the plans until the first of the year because I have already funded my limit this year."

Richard's current net worth is still high even *after* getting mostly wiped out in the 1990s when some of his interest rates went up to 20% and projects were completely shut down.

When he was working 14- to 16-hour days, he wasn't able to do much else besides build his business. "Even if I would have had expensive tastes, I wouldn't have had the time to enjoy them. I would say at the end of the day, reading *Scientific American* is probably the one thing I like to do. I also do some volunteer work in the community in a range of things from a committee for bike paths to suicide prevention."

No surprise here, but he doesn't consider himself a spender, although he does like to spend some to build his own computers. "I do read the figures about what people put away. They say 'try real hard to put away 5, 10, 15%,' so I know what I do is to the extreme. But it is not really discipline, like I said, there is really nothing that I like to buy besides computer gear. Plus, I like investing. I kind of look at that as where I spend my money."

The next step for his first love of science? "Out here [Monterey Bay] we have the Aquarium and Moss Landing Research Station, so those are some of the things I think about getting involved with. I got a phone call recently from the local college saying they want to start up an alcohol and drug treatment certification program and asked for some help. I do want to get involved in something, but I'm in no big hurry to do it. Something will come along that will strike my interest, but right now I'm not spending a whole lot of time thinking about it."

SIX YEARS LATER ...
Net Worth Increased

TIFFANI: You are 60 now. In our first conversation, you were mostly in bonds. You were semi-retired. You were still looking into working with drug and alcohol facilities, but also looking at getting back into sciences. What happened?

RICHARD: Things are pretty much the same, or at least going according to plan. I am still mostly in the bond market.

I did well through the crisis.

I actually made money.

I bought some quality bonds while they were cheap. I was never really expecting to make capital gains on this type of investment, but that's how it turned out. I am still doing the bonds and looking for good opportunities to come along.

I bought another rental property, pretty much near the market low. That was a good opportunity.

I am still keeping my hand in the business. I was doing – and still do – the management consulting. I had one guy doing the daily operations for me. I recently brought in another guy and have been training him for a while. I taught some training in the alcohol and drug field and I did have a private practice, but I've since dropped that.

I am spending a lot more time on personal pursuits. I do enjoy studying the scientific stuff, but also, I've been able to spend time learning about things I had not previously had an opportunity to learn about. I am doing a lot of history. Looking at how we got to be where we are today. Looking at different themes and patterns.

JOHN: I've spent a large bit of my life studying history. What are you currently reading in history?

RICHARD: I watch a lot of documentaries. It kind of started out with a lot of English history. The way you could look at it is that our history – as Americans – prior to 220 years ago, is British history. I've looked at a lot of Islamic history. Some of what I'm studying are things that I had heard about but didn't really understand. Like the Holy Roman Empire, I never really got a handle on what that was and how it came about. Not so much in current history, but I've been learning more about where China is at these days and what sort of development they've had in their systems in the past number of years. A lot of Greek history, especially pre-Hellenic. Again, looking for these recurring themes. A lot on how Empires fall and how they grow and mistakes they made. Reading about it is usually focused on one topic, whereas from a series of documentaries on one subject I can get a broader scope of history that way. That's easier than reading a book on this one subject and that one subject. I like a broader view. BBC has a lot of great documentaries, so I've been watching a lot of them on YouTube. There is actually a lot of good stuff on YouTube. I didn't know that. I thought it just had goofy videos, but you can find some quality stuff.

TIFFANI: So with your love of science and watching documentaries, and still managing your money, what does your day look like?

RICHARD: Generally, the first thing I do is check on the markets. I try not to spend more than an hour or two a day on the investments. That varies quite a bit. Sometimes it's like watching paint dry. Kind of like the recent period. The volatility has been low, the market has been pretty flat. We've had a couple of big down days and I was optimistic that there would be some buying opportunities there, but then a day or two later there was another up day.

JOHN: Were you ever a stock investor or have you always concentrated on bonds?

RICHARD: It was about 2003 that I really switched my emphasis; 100% out of stocks to bonds. I made my first stock investment when I was still in college. I had a friend of a friend who was a stockbroker for Paine Webber. I had inherited a little bit of money – so that is where I made my first investment.

Then the recession of the early 1980s hit. The business I was in at the time, things went very poorly financial-wise. So, I didn't do much during the 1980s, but then I started a new business in the early 1990s. I started investing again, mostly in stocks. I don't know how much it existed before then, but the exchange-traded debt is mostly what I do. That is where they take a bond and chop it up to $25 segments and you can trade it like you trade a stock. Some preferreds, some CEFs.

Stocks take a lot of work and a lot of time, and I didn't really have the time when my business was growing very fast. I figured if I could get around an 8% return, that all the extra work for stocks is not worth it. Plus, it is more conservative, and I was starting to get into capital preservation mode at that point any way. That is kind of where I've been since then. I am not trying to make a killing. In fact, my goal is to do inflation, plus a little better. I target around 7.5% or 8%. The main thing is capital preservation.

TIFFANI: So, your income is basically coming from your interest? Or are you still drawing a salary?

RICHARD: I am still getting a significant income from the business. I am still saving money. I still contribute to every way the

	government gives you an opportunity to. I've got a ROTH, an HSA, a 401(k) and a defined benefit plan.
JOHN:	Explain to us what you do with closed-end funds and your rationale.
RICHARD:	I just buy them when I think they're cheap. They got kind of expensive, so I sold some out, but when Bill Gross left PIMCO a few days ago. PIMCO funds took a big hit, so I bought some PTY, which is one I've had on my watch list forever. They are still at pretty good prices. They've come back a little bit, but I would say they are still pretty good.

The rationale is the same as it is for bonds and preferred stock. The goal there is to get the interest income and to try and buy at a good price.

JOHN:	So you are buying closed-end funds that pay a dividend or yield and you are trying to buy below NAV?
RICHARD:	I look more at the premium – or that is one of the metrics I look at. You want to look at yield, their leverage, the premium or discount over the NAV that they are currently selling at, and then you want to look historically. Those are the things I look at. Leverage is important, but the goal is the same. It's just another form of income investing.
JOHN:	You made your millionaire mark primarily by saving money. No big hits.
RICHARD:	The life I chose was an entrepreneur. I read a book in high school, and it happened to talk about how most of the people you know historically as having been very rich, almost all went broke and most went broke several times before they made it. I always knew I would have ups and downs. My first business did really well and then in the early 1980s it went bad. I then rebuilt things and did something new. I didn't hit the lottery or anything like that, but my first business did make a lot of money really fast. This time, to make $1,000,000 a second time was a lot slower. There is a book called *The Millionaire Next Door*. I never read that book, but I saw descriptions of it. I would say that is kind of where I'm at. I have taken

some flyers on stocks. Most of my net worth is saving and trying to invest prudently. Trying to make a big hit in the market is like going to Vegas and thinking you're going to hit that slot machine. It happens. You hear about it, but it's rare.

What did you hear about finances when you were younger?
We have all the money we need, but no money to waste. Be conservative, but don't be stingy.

What was your best mistake?
I made a bad investment with someone, but it taught me a lot about business. Whether it was dishonest or not, it was worth the cost.

What one thing have you learned about life that you would want written down?
Play Monopoly or poker with money for small stakes, and you will learn more about human nature than any other way.

Favorite books
Age of the Moguls; *The Teachings of Don Juan*; *Sense and Sensibilia* (John Austin); *Crack the Cosmic Ego*; any book by Roger Penrose.

SIX *MORE* YEARS LATER ...
Net Worth Doubled

Here we are again, and Richard is still working in the same business he had been trying to semi-retire from. "I didn't think I would be doing that. I had thought that I would eventually turn the business over to the guy who was working with me. Well, life, he had an intense divorce, kids involved … he had to stop working for me completely. I went back to work full-time. It took another two years to train someone again and set them up in the business the way I want it."

He took the pandemic market as a huge buying opportunity in stocks, to just sit back and watch what happens. He is still heavily in bonds. "I seem to do well in bonds. I am guessing because they are more straightforward and analytical. The only thing you need to figure out is if they are going to stay in business. You don't have to worry about whose product is going to be the most popular and that kind of stuff. If you have some candidates in mind, you keep an eye on them. Wait for something to drive the prices down that hopefully doesn't affect that company individually. You can pick some pretty good prices based on that.

"I will watch the downturns and load up some more on stocks. When you buy on the way down and not try to pick a bottom, your average price is probably going to be well below where it is before it recovers. I don't try to pick bottoms, but I don't want to miss the boat either. It is more of a, 'Hey, am I happy with this price? OK, I will buy it,' even though I know it might not be the bottom of the basket.

"I have more than enough to cover my expected lifetime. Once I am up above a certain point, it all starts to look the same. I don't have any kids or anything, so it all goes to charity. It just depends on how lucky I am. I have thought about having a funnel into a preexisting foundation that has similar charities to what I might pick if I was trying to choose myself."

In all of the choice points in his life – choosing to change his major, choosing to not continue in a career he was burnt out on, choosing to save a jaw-dropping amount – what is his process to make important decisions?

"As you might expect, I'm pretty analytical, but you still have to rely on your gut instinct a lot to know what feels right, and what doesn't. Sometimes there are just so many indefinite things. I have to try to make a decision or get input from other people.

I've been watching a video about Egypt. And apparently, the expression 'two heads are better than one' dates back to at least 1300 BC, because they have that expression, too. So, yeah, I try to get feedback from other people and different points of view, especially if it's a personal decision. Unless it's something I have got to make a quick decision on, I won't rush into it. I'll let it cook on the back burner for a while."

Our enquiring minds wanted an example of following his gut. His answer did not disappoint. It may be one of our favorite snippets.

"Well, during one period. I was actually sleeping in my car, for a variety of reasons. It wasn't necessarily financial. It was a transition of, 'I don't want to be here, do I want to be there?'

"One evening I had been drinking, and so I was sleeping in my car. I have since come to learn you can get arrested for drinking and driving without actually driving, just sleeping under the influence is enough to get you arrested. I was just lying down in the front seat but being arrested does not mean that you are guilty. It just means that you got arrested. So, this cop asks if I want to take a sobriety test. Well, he didn't ask me. I said that there was no point. I'll admit I have been drinking, probably over. He said that if you admit it, then there is no reason to take the test, but they were going to take me in. He tells me I should hire a public defender, that I should probably just cop to this and plead guilty. I just *felt* that, no, I didn't want to do that. I'll go to a rehab sort of thing and I asked the judge. The judge said 'OK, that is fine, report back that you're getting some help.' Now, if I hadn't listened to my gut to not take this cop's advice, it probably would have meant more money and some jail time and a record."

We couldn't help but see the connection to this rehab stint in his 20s and his comments about knowing a bit about the industry. Richard took something a lot of people could have seen as a negative, learned from it, and then an opportunity came along to use it in business.

"I guess the combination of the rehab, finding something I like to do … I just lost interest in the drinking and realized that was the way it needed to be.

"By assisting people, hopefully fewer people have died on the highways. Most of the people who test positive don't have a problem. Most of them just partied too hard last weekend, or at a high level. What the field has tried to do over the years is to raise the bottom. You don't have to be drunk and broke in an alley. Let's try to get to it sooner. That is true for any problem. If you think you are getting sicker, go to the doctor. It is much easier to fix something when it hasn't metastasized."

Richard has said in a few different ways he just doesn't have a lot of wants or hobbies that would take money. We asked if his lifestyle had changed with doubling his net worth.

"Now, I know you keep bringing up lifestyle. I did treat myself to one thing. I bought a classic car a while back, which I hear guys my age do about this time of life. It is a cobalt blue '66 Thunderbird. It has the old sequential left and right turn signal. When you put your turn signal on it goes blink, blink, blink or cross. I have always liked T-birds for as long as I can remember."

This of course got John (a man of that age) talking cars and asking about hardtops, extended engines …

"Definitely hardtop. It is there, I've hardly had a chance to drive it as the guy I am working with, we are all involved with the door. It is in excellent shape. I don't know a thing about classic cars, and you can get ripped off. But there was this guy at this kind of classic car museum. And there was a car that said, 'on loan from,' and those are usually permanent installations. This guy loaning it was getting older and wanted to sell it to somebody who wanted to drive it, use it, and enjoy it.

"Now that things have lightened up a bit at work, I plan to get back to that. They have some very nice car shows around here and I may see if I enjoy going to those and taking the car, just taking it for a spin once in a while. Playing with the engine is another engineering thing. I didn't get the biggest one. I think it is a 398. It is kind of a luxury sports car for the T-birds with an all black interior. Getting into buying these classic cars is a whole thing in itself. I certainly hope I do not end up becoming like Jay Leno and have a whole warehouse for the cars. I am hoping I don't get addicted."

We had to then evil-ask what his next car will be.

"I hope I won't … but then again you get tantalized by certain things. You think, 'Gee, isn't that cool? You know, that would be kind of nice. Well, I guess two is not too many.' That is how it happens.

"Well, I mean it is the only thing I want. So, it is not as though I deprived myself. But this one. I liked it. So I bought it. But everything else I desire was also obtained."

It is hard to relay how the whole tone of Richard's voice changed while talking about this car. His rhythm and excitement came through.

In the background John was discreetly googling this car and started asking about the 'whole shooting-match of the beauty' sitting right there. Richard caved in and revealed that, yes, he did have another car in mind.

"I had been thinking an Avanti might be interesting. That is not your family vehicle. I always loved the DeLorean. Even before that movie, I liked the design of that car."

Where do we stand with the numbers? Richard was worth $1.5 million at our first conversation. Almost 100% in bonds. His net worth has more than doubled.

Income-wise, Richard still hasn't touched his savings. As we know from his chosen hobbies (well, we will have to check back in now that the classic car hobby has been added to the list), the business provides much more than he needs. Each year he stuffs more money into the retirement accounts, and that also helps his taxes. We pressed him a bit on what he enjoys most out of these hobbies.

"I just learn about things. I hope to travel more. I spent time down in the islands in my first career when I was younger. It was in the travel business. I spent a lot of time taking people on junkets to the Caribbean. So, I have been all over the islands down there, learning about business. It is just something that was always second nature to me. I spent a lot of time helping companies and starting my business. I have been doing it for 25 years. I never thought that would happen, but it is different every day. That is a good thing. I liked it better when I had a guy working for me. I still like computer stuff, building my own computers. It is like a giant adult Lego set. I am always updating components, reading what other people are doing, keeping up on that technology. At heart, I am just your average geek.

"When I was in high school, I read a book called *The Age of Moguls*, which was about Morgan, Vanderbilt, all those guys. It was a really interesting book, but almost every one of them went broke at some point. Some of them, multiple times before they became wealthy. So, I already had the mindset that if you're going to be the entrepreneurial type, sometimes you are going to go broke. After the early '80s recession, I was essentially broke. I was prepared and it didn't bother me all that much. I figured this is the lifestyle I chose. I am going to be up, and I am going to be down, but it is not like being an employee. I don't think that was ever something I wanted to do, go into the same job day after day.

"Most of the things I have done, I didn't do for the money. Money has always been kind of secondary. Most people seem to come to that later in life."

QUESTIONS FROM OUR OTHER MILLIONAIRES

What is important to you and how has that changed over time?
I don't think it has changed much; you know me. Find something you enjoy doing and do it. You know, that is what I always hear when I am listening to someone or watching a biography on YouTube. If you like drawing and doing cartoons. If you like woodworking, if you like running a business ... you can usually find a way to make money at it. To get philosophical, that is what it comes down to. That has always been the way it is for me.

I think what might have changed is its degree of significance, because your loved ones are the most important thing in your life. I have had a few people pass away. We should be grateful to just be alive. I have had a lot of blessings to count. You can always look and see somebody worse off than you are. Be grateful for what you have got, not focused on what you don't have.

Were there any significant turning points in your life, in hindsight?
There have certainly been significant experiences that I've learned a lot from. I always felt and believe firmly that people should travel and get outside of their little world and that, you know, in the United States, there's a lot more going on than what happens there. My father was a pretty sharp guy. We just got in the family station wagon every summer and drove. We went to this part of the United States or that part of the United States. We'd be gone anywhere from a few weeks to a couple of months. By the time I was 15, I had been in every one of the 48 contiguous states. I thought that was great. And we didn't travel in a hurry. That is where you are going to see the people and the culture. Always take the back roads.

Quotes to Ruminate On

MOST IMPORTANT LIFE LESSONS FROM THE MOUTHS OF MILLIONAIRES

"Achieving your goal is not a continuous forward journey. Not only are there the usual setbacks, but also planned seemingly backward steps." —Rocky

"It's not what you make; it's what you keep." —Desmond

"Do not spend what you do not have. Do not invest what you cannot lose." —Jacki

"Most important lessons for me are if something sounds too good to be true, it probably is. Also, stick with businesses you know." —Lowery

"Putting all my eggs in one basket when I was younger. I traded gold and lost everything that I inherited from my mom passing. I learned to diversify." —Kevin

"Focus, hard work, and fiscal restraint. Anyone can do well in good times but surviving them in down turns is key." —Al

"Learn how to be thrifty and sometimes downright frugal." —Robert

"No matter how bad things get, they can and will change. My goal for myself and my family is to help them change for the better. Also,

(continued)

marry someone with the same financial values as you have, and stay married." —Tracie

"If after some reasonable analysis, it feels right – trust your instinct. —Desmond

"Do what you said you were going to do." —Mel

"Don't worry too much, the things that will damage in life are likely to be things not foreseen." —William

CHAPTER 3

Never Let a Bad Situation Get the Best of You

GORDON K.
Net Worth: $8–10 Million
Income: $1 Million
Started Investing: 35
Attained Millionaire Status: 52

For some, that entrepreneurial spirit shows itself from a young age. This was definitely the case for Gordon. This kiddo, by the age of 10, had a variety of jobs from selling cool drinks at racetracks to delivering newspapers. "My Dad was a sort of spendthrift and never really put anything back for the family or himself. He hadn't really set much of an example to live up to financially, but rather an example of what not to be.

"I would go off on my moped about 4:45 in the morning and deliver newspapers in Cape Town. My route took me from lower-middle-class areas near my home to the upper-class areas of Bishop Courts, where the *real* money lived. Obviously, trolling through their yards and gardens at that time in the morning and seeing the wealth, the Maserati parked on two acres of land instead of a quarter acre, it showed me up close and personal how the 'other side' lived. I don't know why we didn't have much money, but we were always just scraping things together when I was a kid.

"I knew who I did *not* want to be like. I saw the folks who lived in the ritzy neighborhoods. Envy was the great motivator for me to work hard and get ahead. I always had a competitive spirit, but that ignited it.

At times I would say, 'I wish I could ...' and Dad would reply, 'You can, son!'"

He attributes stick-to-itiveness, being a team builder and a great listener as the character traits to building his success. "I think I made the decision that if I choose something that I like, I *was* going to be good at it and give it my all. The same applied later in my life when I started in business."

Gordon left his home in South Africa in his early twenties with the dream of breaking into filmmaking. He had been working with and for his father on a film and television crew covering a lot of African events. In fact, his last job before he left that industry was as a cameraman and stringer for NBC. This was in the days of film, before video was around.

"I had a friend down there who had done very well making commercials for American companies and I sort of wanted to go on the same track. I had some training from a technical school in Cape Town, plus I had about two year's experience in the field. I wanted to get into the London Film School. We had some connections with some movie people who had come to Cape Town to shoot various movies. I got an introduction to the school and actually went there for three or four weeks.

"It was really expensive and, given the time I had spent in the field, I knew pretty much everything they were going to teach me, or so I thought. (In our early twenties that is the way it was.) But film schools of the late 1960s and early '70s are nothing like the film schools of today. That didn't pan out, but what did is that I actually met an American girl and we started dating and she invited me to come to the states on a vacation with her."

She became his wife and he ultimately moved to the United States permanently. "At that time, I was still a stringer for NBC back in South Africa. I called NBC New York to see if I could transfer there for work, but I didn't have any associations with the unions, and because of this, couldn't join them.

"Interesting sidenote: They did offer me a job in Vietnam as a film cameramen. They actually offered it to me several times because their cameraman kept being shot up and they were running out of them. I could have done that, and it would have given me a ticket to the union once back in the United States, but it was a two-year stint."

The American girl did not approve of two years away, and it did not materialize.

His last time in London he worked a basket of odd jobs – a bus driver for a grocery chain, working at the Mars Bars factory making Mars Bars, and putting down rails for the monorail cranes. Interestingly enough, these odd jobs in London added up to a two-year stint, but all that time still able to date his American girl.

"I got bored and saw I wasn't going anywhere, so I decided to go back to South Africa and see what I could find there. I was homesick anyway, so I went back. I left my girl in London to get into the movie business in South Africa. She decided to follow me six weeks later, and we ultimately got married there."

Now, his wife was from New Jersey. What does a boy born and raised in South Africa know about Jersey? Not very much, he tells us. It was part of the package deal and when they finally moved to the States, it was to New Jersey near her family.

In retrospect, Gordon calls it luck that defined some of his success today. His wife's parents wanted her to come home and didn't like her living in South Africa. To help sweeten the deal, her father invited Gordon to come back to the States with her and he would organize a job for him. "All the while, I really wanted to go back and pursue my photography/filmmaking career. We decided we had nothing to lose in moving and could fall back on South Africa."

His father-in-law, a fundraiser by profession, had a small packaging business. They packaged toiletry products for various charities, including the American Red Cross and the Salvation Army.

He needed some help. He wanted Gordon to run the business, so he could focus full-time on raising funds.

"He put me in the basement of his house. Sat me down at a desk with a telephone and just said, 'Here, run this thing.'

"I would solicit samples from the likes of Colgate, Gillette, Pepsodent, and big manufacturers. We were putting together 300,000–400,000 packages a year with distribution to kids who were going off to Vietnam. I coordinated with a lot of inbound shipments coming in from manufacturers and the packaging of them for the organizations. They would then take possession of the goods and distribute them to the troops as they left the assembly stations. I did that for six years."

During that time a consultant, brimming with an interesting story and character, turned into his mentor. "Bernie was a very successful man in his own right. He started life in an orphanage in Boston. He moved up the ranks as a male secretary and ended up as one of the division presidents at Gillette. He was a very savvy fellow with a good philosophy of business and how to get things done. Working with him was exciting and it taught me an awful lot.

"I consider those years as my Manhattan MBA; Bernie was glad to pass this on. We pounded the pavements of Fifth Avenue, and everyone loved him. He was retired and not doing much and he saw me as a project, I guess. So, he conveyed and passed on to me his business philosophy. It was a privilege to work with him.

"Now, this had nothing to do with filmmaking and, with a wife and child, I was desperate to just make a living. I was more interested in putting bread on the table than pushing any artistic career."

Gordon professes that one of his life lessons was to never let a bad situation get the best of you. Let's backtrack to one of these instances with his father-in-law. (They will keep coming.) "Here is one situation. In the early 1980s, I was in California. I had pretty much flown out there on a wing and a prayer to try and help my father-in-law expand his operation. I wasn't making terribly good money. I was making $25,000 to $30,000 a year. While I was out there, he decided to sell the company."

Hearing he was going to sell the company left him cold. "I said, 'Oh my goodness, what are we going to do now?' I saw the accountant coming in, sharpening a pencil, and saying that we don't need this, this, and this, and we can dump this whole operation and bingo! Gordon is stuck out on the west coast with no job.

"Ultimately, that deal fell apart around the lawyer's table at closing. At that time, he decided he wanted me back in New Jersey. I was told he did still plan to sell the company, but he didn't like who was going to run it. He wanted me back to run the whole company. He gave me a little bit of an incentive, more pay, and I did it."

After two more years, he started to get disgruntled. His father-in-law had gone on a tear buying a horse farm, a limousine company, a restaurant, and expensive playthings. Gordon felt like he was funding and supporting all of that by running the company. They ultimately had a few run-ins and one day he was told bluntly that he was overpaid, that as owner, his father-in-law was in his rights to do what he was doing, and that Gordon needed to be a "good boy" and sit down and be quiet. "Well, that didn't sit well and I started exploring the possibility of breaking away and starting my own company."

Even though the family situation was an absolute mess, Gordon relays the father was alienating others in the family and ultimately one of his other children committed suicide. "It was shortly after this death that I had simply had enough. This man was taking advantage of me. He was making in excess of $600,000 a year. I was making $65,000."

Once an entrepreneur, always an entrepreneur. In the accumulated years of experience, he had noticed potential opportunities the company had not taken or had ignored. He had seen that there was a market for first responders and disaster relief. He saw tremendous potential there. He had mentioned this before, but his father-in-law had "poo-pooed" it, not wanting to put money into it.

Gordon went for it. He started with disaster response kits and then created a company that makes emergency-response trailers. "Once I finally said that I am going to leave and start this, it made things all the more easy. There was a market out there that was almost untapped and so I went after it quite solidly. We have done well here since.

"We do medical trailers that would be agile to hospitals in the event of a big disaster. We have developed them for various states. They are 40-foot containers packed with food, water, clothes, blankets, toiletries, and other essentials that victims would have access to in the event of an earthquake or disaster." They also started to work with the State Department to provide family hygiene kits for refugee programs in Africa and Turkey after disasters.

A majority of Gordon's $10 million net worth is tied up in his business, which he acknowledges his financial advisors say is too much. "I probably have retained earnings in the business in excess of $3.5–4 million. Right now, we are carrying about $2 million in accounts receivable and about $1.5 million of inventory, with about $800,000 cash. Most of my net worth is in ProPack." However, he does own commercial and residential real estate. "I have an old movie theater complex I bought. I gutted it and made a warehouse and my office out of it. Wonderful building, it really is. It is about 20,000 square feet. I actually just put it up for sale and have about $1 million of my net worth tied up in that. I have another small warehouse, and a home down in South Africa."

He stays far away from the stock market after watching one of his investments whittle away to nothing. Remembering how he grew up paycheck-to-paycheck, Gordon saves about $150,000 a year to make sure he always has enough.

He has a penchant for collecting cars. On the high end, a Ferrari 575 Maranello, fairly new Morgan, six or seven Porsches, an arrangement of Mini Coopers from the 1970s and '80s, a '53 Chevy pickup, and a '57 Barris coupe customized by George Barris for Ringo Starr. His car collection alone is worth about $1.7 million.

He regrets not talking to his children more about finances. "I should have been far more proactive at the beginning of my divorce, and I really wasn't. I should have just said I am going to keep you close to me and this is how it is going to be. It has only been years later I have seen the consequences of my inaction. I tried to be the nice guy and make sure the kids were not any more hurt than they already were. I would say not spending enough time with my kids was something I regret."

SIX YEARS LATER ...
Net Worth Decreased to $6–7 Million

JOHN: Gordon, what a pleasure to speak again. Let's just dig in. You are 66 now. You were doing emergency response trailers. You had a net worth of $5–10 million. You were making about a million a year, then the recession hit. How were you positioned at the time and what happened to you?

GORDON: I personally fell prey to the skyrocketing property market. I had managed to hold my own and resist any of the temptation to dabble and buy into any of those fast-appreciating properties. We had seen a lot of that in Charleston. I have lived in Charleston, SC, 30 years now and have watched this place turn around. There was a lot of speculation going on with property.

Over the years, I had missed buying some waterfront property several times because I was too conservative. I didn't think it was worth what it was. Then I saw the property values escalating at the rates that they did, and I was still standing on the sidelines.

I thought, if not now, when? I was financially comfortable. I was making good money and the business was doing well.

However, I didn't look far enough down the road. If it sounds and looks too good to be true, it is. I put all that extra in and it *was* cash.

Then the recession hit, and wow, property values just plummeted. Having my house appraised now, the $1 million that I put into it doesn't even show up. I am lucky to get, in my property, what I paid for it unimproved in late 2006.

That is the story over and over again. I have a friend that was so impressed with our property that he later bought a 25-acre farm right on the river. It was on the market for $1.65 million. He picked it up for $600,000. Down the river from us there is a gentleman that built a huge compound on about 8 acres with two houses. It had $7–8 million in it and it sold at auction for $2.4 million.

TIFFANI: That is a big adjustment to fall prey too. How did it affect your business?

GORDON: At the beginning, we were still doing very well. We were stuck in the aftermath of Katrina, which was good for us. There was a knee-jerk reaction from all the government and humanitarian agencies to stockpile to the point where they should have been pre-Katrina. There was a lot of hindsight. "We weren't ready, but we'll be ready next time. Let's go and buy all this stuff." Business was really good. I think our sales in the aftermath of that was around $20–25 million a year for several years.

Then the Great Recession hit, and we probably dropped to $10–12 million. Now we are crawling our way back doing $8 million a year. We'll get to 10 and 12 fairly soon, but we are seeing a slow, moderate growth and recovery. It is certainly not like the good old days. We took a hit and several of our competitors went out of business, which, in the end, helped us a little bit.

JOHN: Kind of the last-man-standing effect?

GORDON: It is. We were kind of the creators of this business. I have been in the business for 25 years and 10 years prior to that working for someone else. I am well versed and experienced in the business.

Over time I have had a lot of copycats. I can go to competitor's websites and can read copy that *I* wrote 20 years ago that they lifted. Even the names of kits that I have copyrighted, but it's just not worth the time and money to sue the bastards.

JOHN: I remember the year after our interview, I went to dinner with a longtime friend of mine. I asked how he was doing, and I expected to hear a real tale of woe. I knew his business had to be dying. He said, "Well, all our competitors have gone out of business and we're the last guys." Even though his business was down, he got the market. He was the last guy standing.

GORDON: For us too, there was a double jeopardy here. Pre-2008, Red Cross used to be one of our biggest customers. In a bad year, we would do a few million dollars with them. In an average year, we would do $3–5 million. We had a great relationship. Well in comes a new president and she is going to sweep clean and bring political correctness right to the forefront. She fired a lot of managers and brought in a lot of other managers. Some of them were competent and some were not. Unfortunately, the ones that got appointed to our account were not. So, with this new crew in Charlotte where all the buying is done, I went up there with my managers and did a great song and dance with the video and slideshow presentation of what we do and how we do it. At the end they basically said, "We really don't need you anymore. We have FedEx and Walmart." That was it. Since then, we've probably done less than $100,000 of business with them. We were shoved out the door. Besides that, the business is still doing well, and we are still making money.

JOHN: Is your net worth – apart from your house being down a million – doing OK? You are still working, so is your net worth where it was?

GORDON: No it's not. My net worth is down quite a bit. I probably lost $300,000–$400,000 in the stock market.

Very foolishly, I spent a lot of money in a two-and-a-half-year period, on estate planning. I had a tax attorney, a CPA, and a financial advisor. When I met with them, the hourly cost was about $1,250.

The upshot of that and hindsight tells me exactly how this industry works now. They are going to pump you so full of sunshine, they make you feel you are the nicest, wealthiest guy in the world, and you need to cover your ass.

The basis of all of this at the end of it was I had to buy myself a $6 million life insurance policy at the cost of about $180,000 a year. I did that. That policy is in effect today.

JOHN: Is it something you plan to keep in effect?

GORDON: It is, but what I did was that I spent over $500–$600,000 on this policy to keep it in effect. I realized it was so over-inflated that it's ridiculous.

I called the agent, and I said what is the value of the policy today if I froze it and made no further payments. It's a paid-up policy until age 121. I asked how much insurance I had. He looked it up and said I would have $1.3 million of insurance and I told him to do that. I'm not paying another dime. By the way, the financial consultant on the front end of this got $80,000 commission.

I ended up putting together what they call an IDGT – Intentionally Defective Grantor's Trust. What it does is it freezes at a fairly low level of your net worth or the worth of your business. The date we chose was August 19, 2009. It is expensive, you have to have an audit and a CPA do an evaluation of the business. But what the IDGT does is it freezes all those values. They do not go up as the value of the business or other assets go up. If you do the projections on that, it could be a $5–15 million tax savings. You do a letter to the IRS, saying this is what we've done, sign off on it. Oh, by the way, you've challenged this five times and lost in court every time. They wrote back and said go for it and that is what we did. That was a very sophisticated tax strategy. It doesn't help me now, but it will help my heirs.

JOHN: What do you think your net worth is now?

GORDON: I would say it is probably between $6 and $7 million. It had been as high as $14 million. The other thing I'll mention is in 2005, I bought a house in South Africa. When I bought the house, the exchange rate was 5 rand to the dollar. I made a deposit in my South African checking account late last week and the exchange rate was 11.28.

JOHN: Your business is doing well, so your monthly income is enough, and you are still saving?

GORDON: To be honest, I am not saving anything. My income is sufficient to support me. I travel a great deal. I just spent the month of August in South Africa and will go back again in December.

The kid who took the brunt of this is my son. He joined me 9 years ago and was a Navy pilot. He was in the Navy for 13 years. He joined me and the plan we wrote at the time had him making really good money 10 years down the road. Unfortunately, he hasn't reached that. He's making decent money, about a couple of hundred thousand dollars a year plus benefits.

However, our plan called for him to be making twice that. That hasn't happened, but we are on a forward growth road. We have some great new products and kicked some more unprofitable products to the curb. We are concentrating on a new line of inflatable buildings for emergency hospitals, and we've done really well with them.

TIFFANI: Oh, I finally get to slide in a question about your son. He is still in the business with you and doing well, you said, other than the income stream adjustment?

GORDON: Yes, but I think he needs his head read. He got married in December. He had already had two young daughters and married a young lady with three young daughters. He is living in a house with six females. The kids are in the range of 7 to 12 years old. He married a nice girl. She is a nephrologist and very well respected. They suit each other, but five girls. (All of this is said lightheartedly.)

The plan is that he is going to take over. To be honest, I'm downsizing. I refinanced the business and the properties that I own and consolidated a lot.

We kind of got ourselves into a bind during the recession. I had a $2 million credit line and as times got tough, we dipped into the credit line. All of a sudden, the bank I was with got bought. The new crew moved in and said we are knocking you down from $2 million to $1 million and you have to come up with the rest. We had a little bit of cash, and I threw that at it. Then I had to remortgage the business building we are in. Fortunately, I had $700,000–$800,000 of equity so that paid off the credit line. They then reduced the credit line to $750,000. That has been that way for a year, and we haven't touched it.

TIFFANI: What a ride the past six years have been, and you are remarkably positive about it all. Let's think about your son, what is the one thing you have learned about life that you would want passed down?

GORDON: It is not the "things" – it is the people and the experiences. Today is the tomorrow you planned for yesterday! Do something with it!

What has changed in your life as a result of achieving millionaire status?
I'm a lot less aggressive and listen more. I have more confidence in myself and want to pass that on to others.

Most important life lesson
Be adaptable, roll with the punches, never let a bad situation get the better of you. Think, think, think, and smile a lot. Having a good command of the English language with good writing skills.

Favorite books
The Last Lion trilogy on Winston Churchill; biographies of successful tycoons of the late 1800s and early 1900s.

SIX *MORE* YEARS LATER ...
Net Worth Increased Upwards of $50 Million

Well, this time catching up with Gordon he came in hot, juggling "six glass balls in the air," as he told us first thing. We left Gordon with a plan to grow his company's bottom line back, and to get his son on track to make the income and plan they had set for him and the business.

First glass ball in the mix was that his son wound up leaving the company and starting his own business. He had been a Navy pilot and went back to flying.

"He is now a drone pilot, doing drone photography and surveying. He is busier than ever. We are still on great terms. He felt more comfortable paddling in his own canoe. I am very proud of him; he is doing it very well and is in high demand. The irony of this is that, had he still been with us, we would not be where we are today. I would have relaxed more."

We can tell you from his previous interviews and the warmth when he talks about his son that he is very proud of him. He relays a story of something that, as every father hopes to see, principles he taught his son made a difference in his life.

"We were always very keen on sports. He turned out to be very, very good at soccer. Since he was in eighth grade, he played on the first team and was also the placekicker on the football team. He had great exposure and got three scholarship offers to college.

"I believe it was the time and energy he put into soccer, as well as the dedication and discipline that came with it, and I was behind him, that made a difference in his life. I used to be his soccer coach back in the day, and that stayed with him for a very long time.

"I laid the groundwork for my kids, that you can do anything you want to do. You just have to put your mind to it.

"I used myself as an example, as you know, I didn't come from much. My folks didn't have any money. They could not afford to send me to college. I sort of had to fend for myself, on my own. He did too, but luckily, he desired to be a Navy pilot. He wanted to be Top Gun, with Tom Cruise and all that stuff. He went to the Naval Academy. He was one of 52 appointments that year and he stayed there. He got his degree in ocean engineering and went to flight school.

"Unfortunately, he was jet-qualified, but they ran out of jet money. So, all 12 of his classmates in his squadron got helicopters. Serendipitously, he never would have jumped ship to come work with me if he had been flying jets. He would have continued in the Navy. The best we could do is when he did join us, we bought an airplane, so he was still able to fly."

Financially, there was once again some issues with a bank and credit line, but with some "hard work and selling of some of my hobby collection," they managed to come out okay. "We have got a super team here. There are about 27 of us now. The title could be: 'Everybody's got a job.' There is not much of a pecking order or hierarchy. It is a real team effort, and I am sort of the coach."

What does it mean to not have a hierarchy? It is not a normal thing to hear from a business owner that everything is running smoothly on a team, that they are a family and flourishing. Just how has he created this environment?

"On a very personal level, it is taking an interest in them and their families, what they are doing, what happened on the baseball field last weekend. Just knowing about them, who went boating, who went jet skiing, who did this or that. It is just like a big family reunion, and it is taking an interest in them on that level. I don't crack the whip around here; I leave that to our CFO. She is the bad cop; I am the nice cop. There is the fact that there is nothing they do that I could not or would not do. My wife is going into the warehouse right now to help pack kits.

"One key player is retired Army Colonel Harry. He was a lecturer at the Citadel and a logistician friend of mine put me together with him and said, 'You need to work with this guy.' He is probably one of the smartest guys I have ever met. He is a walking Excel spreadsheet; he does all that stuff in his head and is just wonderful for us. He was with me for 26 years. When the pandemic hit, he jumped back in with both feet. Not even in his previous position. He did warehouse logistics, shipping, receiving, making sure the hundreds of thousands of boxes that we received got picked, packed, and stacked the correct way. That is actually true. So far, no mistakes. Not that we know of anyway.

"In terms of the pandemic, as you can imagine, it has been good for business.

"I have always defined luck as what happens when opportunity meets preparedness. Well, we have been in the preparedness business for 32 years. It is our mantra that we do all over the country, talking to first responders, public health officials, emergency management agencies, and all the rest of it.

"The idea is that you should be prepared, that you know what you are supposed to be doing, and that there is federal money available to help you do it. So, if you are not prepared, it is your fault. It sounds a little harsh. But there are grants available and we have dedicated our sales efforts to those that need help sprucing up their preparedness plans all over the country. Well, we have been well sourced all over the world for years, so when it hit that everyone needed masks, gloves, sanitizer, we were the lead supplier to the City of New York.

"What changed on a dime was that it was difficult to find funding. The rules changed as the factories started demanding cash up front before shipping anything. It was an incredibly sophisticated endeavor. We had to get good transit, usually by air freight, and the air freight bill had to be paid up front for wheels up. To charter any plane was going to cost $900,000 to $1.4 million, depending on the content and the dimensions.

"We went to the secondary financing market. It was kind of like meeting Guido down in the Bowery and talking to some loan sharks. Interest rates were 35% and 40% for 90-day loans. We were able to get better terms from a few people. With the sudden increase in demand, we were in a position with the vendors of having a track record for years. We were already in play. We had a good list we could go back to and say, 'Look, this isn't our usual order, we need 10 times that,' and they were happy to help.

"For the record, the only way we have let them down is gloves, which turned into a global nightmare for everyone."

All this excitement in Gordon, made us remark that it doesn't sound like he has any plans to slow down. He countered with, "Well, I do, and it is all very hush-hush. I am planning to put it on the market. I have spoken to about five M&A firms and I have narrowed it down to two. I will basically sell the business and reward my key employees after the sale, rewarding them quite handsomely. The idea is to free me up. One of the things you do when you come to a sale like this is selling the future. We have been on a good three- to five-year run and they are not going away. All the stockpiles have been consumed."

And ... the numbers. In our first interview, Gordon was saving about $150,000 a year with a net worth of about $10 million.

Round two revealed there was no opportunity to save, and his net worth had dropped to $6–7 million. Getting us caught up, Gordon is now saving about $1 million a year.

And the final number is ... well, over $50 million. As John would say, "That is a good day at the office."

Remember those cars Gordon told us about? The collection's worth increased to around $3 million.

"I've got a car on the way. I bought a 1930 Bentley in England a couple of months ago. It was about $650,000. I built my dream garage, which was a 20-car garage. I have a motorcycle garage, because I had about 30 collector bikes. But I do drive them all. I have a young man who works for me full-time. He keeps them running and clean. And we are taking delivery of a '65 Porsche convertible tomorrow at 9 a.m., all dressed up, from a real big collector out on the West Coast.

Bruce Mayer is probably one of the most important collectors on the West Coast.

"Let's just say that's where my interest has sort of transferred from the business to some of my little toy hobbies."

We wanted to go a little deeper into his previous mention of locking his estate. Things have changed, some of them heart-wrenching. "We had to create an irrevocable trust. It was done in light of potential taxes for those I leave behind. It made sense at the time. A lot changed.

"I lost my middle son in a jet ski accident in the Keys. That was tough."

Through some very good legal advice and judicious application, his estate attorney (who also happened to have been a probate judge) somehow managed after letters on scores of letters to appeal to the court to change the irrevocable trust to something more beneficial. All in all, it took almost three years to complete the transition and a substantial amount of money for accountants and legal advice. Gordon still has two life insurance policies totaling a smidgen over $2 million. He could cash them in, but in his words, "There is no reason to; with my current situation and net worth, those insurance policies are essentially meaningless in the grand scheme of things."

The longevity view of Gordon's journey through these years reflects what we have seen again and again. He found something in which he could succeed and had to keep at it, through ups and downs, proving that the old adage works, "Never give up." Just how did he keep going when faced with what looked like all signs pointing toward throwing in the towel?

"There were many times when I wanted to give up. I couldn't afford to give up. I owed too much money. I had too many mouths to feed, employees and family. It was a matter of necessity. This is why I knew I couldn't change crafts midstream. I always saw the light at the end of the tunnel. I would just put on a raincoat and bring out the umbrella, and you know, slog through the hard times. In those trying times, I'd advise talking to your fellow business owners. Peel the onion with someone else, suddenly things don't look so bad. It is comforting to know you are not the only one out there."

QUESTIONS FROM OUR OTHER MILLIONAIRES

What is important to you and how has that changed over time?
At this point in my life, what is important to me is the time available. And it's easy for me to say, "Now, you can always make some more money, but you can't make any more time." My time is used, I think, quite wisely. I don't like to waste time. I have things to do, people to meet, and adventures to have.

It's less now about concentrating on the business. I think that's all been well done. Now, my concentration is on divestiture. And what do I do from here? And how can I share this with people that matter to me?

I'm planning some trips next year, international trips that will be quite significant. And I'm inviting friends along with me, and I'll pay their way. And I'm wanting to help my son develop his business. As I said, there's a big chunk waiting for him. I helped my grandkids out. And, you know, I want to share my wealth, literally, and share myself with friends and family. So, you know, time is the biggest asset I have right now. I don't have that much left. I have to use it wisely.

Even how I manage my time has changed over the years. I used to show up at 7:30 a.m. and wouldn't leave until 7 pm and just work, work, work. I still get up at 6 am, I go for a 45-minute walk on the beach, I watch the news and catch up on the newspaper and emails. I use about 45 minutes of "thinking time." Sometimes that is spent on business, sometimes on a hobby, sometimes thinking on family. I find it to be a quiet cushion. This allows me to start my day at 9 a.m., and also allows me to miss rush-hour traffic.

I manage time during the day; for example, if I spent most of the day behind closed doors or at a rotary meeting, that means tomorrow I am going to spend time in the lobby, walking down the halls and talking to people that work for me. You have to make time for that.

(continued)

Were there any significant turning points in your life, in hindsight?

Not so much a turning point, but I didn't give myself sufficient credit. I never felt like I was good enough to be out there with the first-team players when I was younger. If we had matriculation, as we called it back then, and there were classes A, B, C, or D, I was always in the C or D class. I was never at the top of my class. But I always felt that I had abilities as good as anyone there. I didn't stress myself or put myself out there enough to put my head down and just go for it. I was scared of making a fool of myself. I should have done that earlier.

Do you think you are rich?

I would say I am rich financially. But in a way, I feel poor, in a family sense. I am not as close to my family as I would like to be for a lot of different reasons – time, distance, circumstance. So yes, I am rich from a financial perspective. But from a soulful perspective, I am not rich at this; I have a long way to go.

eavesdropping on

Millionaires' Childhoods

"As I think back to my childhood, my Dad taught me the value of education and, secondly, the importance of never quitting. Those two things are probably the most important things I learned. He started half a dozen different small businesses with sort of mediocre success, but he never stopped trying to do it. He taught me the value of hard work, so starting at 10 I had paper routes, collected clothes hangers and sold them to the local cleaning service. My father was a sales manager for a bottling company, so at the ripe old age of about 12, when I wasn't in school, I would ride around with him and listen to what he talked to people about."

—Terry

"My father gave us pocket money but taught us to be disciplined. It was always written into an old-fashioned stock-keeping ledger that I am amazed they still make. It had a balance and debits and credits. You would be credited a certain amount that was indexed to your age every school holiday and half term .... You see, if it was every week (a shorter time period between payments) it would encourage us to buy sweets or small items. We had a large amount at once, but it had to last the whole term or holiday.

You weren't allowed to make the entries in it yourself, and even if we thought we had cleverly gotten the amount off of my mom, my dad would make the entry and calculate what the closing balance

(continued)

was after the complete transaction. We watched him and I always knew exactly what was in my account.

For example, I would have 9 pounds 27 in my account but see a watch that was 8 pounds and know with Dad that I could buy it. Now, if it was 12 pounds, I could probably tell my mom I had 15 pounds and she would give me the 12 pounds, but when I got home Dad would see that and DOUBLE the amount that you overspent and you had to wait till you accumulated that money back to spend more. Yes, the interest was charged to us if we went into debt at extortionist rates. There was no way we could exceed our allowance unless it was a real gift, we couldn't beg for more money. This taught us the importance of budgeting. We all knew that we had money in that ledger, but if we went out and bought a huge box of toys or ate an ice cream every day for two weeks, then we wouldn't have money for the rest of the month."

—William

"Father grew up in the depression and only went through the sixth grade. We were very frugal. I had what I needed, but not always what I wanted. He put a lot of emphasis on education. He was adamant that we go to college and be able to fend for ourselves once got out. He complained about spending money on a lot of things, but he never said a word about spending on education. I could still be going to school today and if he were alive he would still be paying for it."

—Lowery

CHAPTER 4

Creating Your Own Path

From Family Expectations to Personal Fulfillment

RICHARD R.
Net Worth: $1–2 Million
Income: $200–500k
Started Investing: 35

Richard knew from an early age that he was "expected" to enter the family business; and despite a *tiny* issue that it was not on his personal radar, he gave it a noble effort.

"My father had a great mind and was such a unique character, but he was an engineer through and through." His father wanted him to follow in his footsteps; so even though Richard was more interested in economics and business, he still ended up going to college for engineering.

After seven years of playing around, he left school without a degree. "I knew I was not an engineer. I realized I didn't have the personality to go through with it."

Richard's parents had been unable to have children, and he became their son through adoption. He remembers that his parents were very much in love, but emotionally disconnected from him.

His father believed you worked for your money and that people in the financial industry had nothing to add to the world. He was an interesting individual and had a number of patents in his name and inventions that he never got patented.

"I have to tell his story, to tell what he is and how I rebelled against it. He was born in 1921 and his father left his mother at the beginning of the Depression. His dad came back eventually but used to beat the hell out of him. My father was an incredibly controlled individual, so he never beat me, but he was tough nonetheless, in his own way. He was hard to connect with, but we did find some things, like hockey and the business. He was a great engineer. He would grab a problem and wrestle it into submission.

"He had a contracting business, and when I was 14, I started doing sheet metal construction, tin-knocking duct work installation. Then when I was 18, I moved to outside sales and project management. I went through the whole air conditioning industry with the hope by my father that I would be an engineer. He didn't make money based on his relationships with long-term customers and opportunities built that way, which is how I am, and I only learned that after a certain length of time fighting it.

"He hoped I would fill his shoes, which were never the shoes I could fill. It wasn't in my nature. I gave it a try in college. I realized I didn't have the personality that it required. It wasn't my thing. I was more interested ultimately in economics and business, so my time in college I feel was wasted on engineering. I was bright enough to get away with it for a while, but I was fooling myself."

Richard vulnerably shared an experience that he knows had a profound impact on him and part of the reason he stayed in the business with the connection to his father. "The summer I got raped, I basically no longer wanted to be home, so I went to work every day with him. He thought I wanted to be around the business, but I was just terrified to be at home. I am pretty clear that he misinterpreted my staying close to the business and my looking to him as being interested in the business. I was never able to talk about it and I was never able to talk about it to anyone in the family; it was a real problem in the end."

His journey from reluctant employee who had started just wanting to feel safe to successfully running the family business was a rocky one. When Richard was in college, his father was looking at retirement from his HVAC business, and Richard just wasn't ready. "I thought that I was, and had wanted to be. I just wasn't. I was still in school and I was just poking around and I took the seven-year plan to not even get a degree."

His father ended up handing the reins to a man who essentially ran the business into the ground and ruined his retirement and wealth. "So, at that time, we started a second company. I told him I didn't really want to do this [a running theme]. But this was his lifeboat. I learned a great deal from my father during those years. I learned how to close a company and deal with the IRS and all sorts of interesting things at the age of 25. Stuff that I really shouldn't have had to learn, but it was good for me nonetheless."

Knowing the business was only going to get worse, Richard and his dad decided to divide the company. "With the first business, we had 80 employees and an overhead of $7 million, except the company was only doing $4 million of work a year. So, we took the service side of the business, which was always my father's baby, and set up a separate company with me as the president. I figured what the hell, it will only be three years. Then I kept saying to myself, 'Five years, where will I be in five years?' I would imagine that and push through." He admits that at the time he was self-medicating a great deal, but thinks it was probably the thing that kept him alive.

The direction of the business changed in 1993 when his father got a patent for an HVAC widget, the device they continue to sell to this day. His father created an ad and was sure he was going to get thousands of leads and when he didn't, he was crushed.

He wouldn't have continued, but Richard stepped in and told him that he could make it work. They decided to close up the other business and focus solely on selling the new widget. Richard made some sacrifices and even went on unemployment, and for three years they worked hard on building the company. "I basically waited tables on the side and pulled what little I had from savings, doing everything I could to get it off the ground."

Working that closely with his father, the writing was on the wall, and it took a toll on their relationship. After three and a half years, he finally realized it was useless and counterproductive for them to work together in such close proximity. "We didn't see eye to eye. He was the dictator of the business, and I couldn't take it anymore. It was hard to connect with him in a lot of ways because of his upbringing and abuse he suffered as a young man. I said, 'Screw it, I am going.' That definitely changed our relationship."

He completely left the company, moved all the way to a different state and worked construction for a few years in Boston. Then his Dad called and said he was ill, and to come back ... again. As a marine, his Dad had been hit by a rifle butt in a riot in Cuba and he hadn't gotten proper medical care. He suffered a collapsed forehead and other issues and was now experiencing enormous pain and trouble with his head.

"I said I won't come back to work or back to Connecticut, but I will do the sales and marketing from Boston. I didn't have a piece of the company and I wasn't very well paid. I kind of skated through for another few years."

In his second go-around with the company, Richard focused on sales and marketing and found they were much more his niche. A few years later his Dad finally officially retired, and told him to take over the company. Richard moved all the operations to Massachusetts. The company has seen steady growth ever since, and now, three years after the move, does over $1 million a year in business.

Despite that, Richard still doesn't love it. "For the most part it is far too solitary and not something I really enjoy doing. This isn't a product that you go door to door selling. You have to build a network and you have to get on the road. When I was younger it wasn't so much of a problem, but now it seems harder to move myself."

His father recently passed away, and Richard is conflicted as to whether he will stay in the business or get out. "I started seeing a therapist a few years ago. It was the best thing I could have ever done for myself; I found the right guy. So he and I are working on how I focus so I can get out. I am actively looking at building an exit strategy for leaving the business at the right time so that I can go on to bigger and better things. I'll probably need to grow into different market segments that I haven't focused on in the past. I am hoping this current economic environment will allow me to do that."

Richard is conservative and has somewhere in the range of a quarter of a million dollars in gold and another $60,000–$70,000 in a bullion vault. He also has a trading account that totals about $250,000 and some other money in an IRA. Richard has been experimenting with options, as he wants to find a way to short the market. Unfortunately, he didn't realize that he had set a sell parameter to automatically sell in case he wasn't around, and he missed half the run on one deal. Lesson learned.

"Probably the reason my company has not grown as much as maybe it should have, is that I have spent a fair amount of my time learning about investing from people like you, John, learning what my options are, and learning how to protect my assets. I started reading and I realized investment advisors and counselors available at my level were woefully inadequate, and they would tell me the most cliché things. So, I had to figure out what I wanted to do."

Richard 100% wants to sell his business down the line. There is a market, he believes, he hasn't even tapped yet. "Theoretically, there are 60 million air conditioners on the roofs of buildings all over; if I can sell to 10% of them, that would be optimistic, but it would make my business 10 times as large. If I put in two to five years, it will be worth a great deal more."

When asked about savings, Richard says there's not much to tell. "To be honest I haven't saved a lot of my money through this period. I just took over the company three years ago. The company is doing very well now, and I'm putting a lot of my earnings away fast because of my concerns about the economy. I have put money aside and haven't wasted it living the high life. My favorite things to spend money on are experiences and not physical items."

"I kind of always understood about money. I always knew I would make money. I never questioned it. Maybe it was my Mom blowing smoke up my butt for the first 40 years of my life, that I am just the golden boy. I actually never thought twice about it, and it was never hard to make money. Even when I wasn't making a lot of it, I knew that I could survive on what I was making, and I would make more. I never doubted that."

SIX YEARS LATER ...
Net Worth Increased to $3.5 Million

JOHN: Last time we talked, it didn't seem you were that happy. You're 50 years old now. What's happened in the last six years, and how are you doing?

RICHARD: At the time I was running a business that was small, and it required my constant vigilance and energy. That was basically getting me to the point where I was not sure it was what I wanted to continue doing. Since then, I have restructured, or rather built the business up. I reached a point where I hired help, and the company has continued to succeed. I am less involved in the day-to-day minutiae and the irritants.

JOHN: That is giving you more of the fulfillment that you were hoping to find?

RICHARD: I don't remember exactly what I said six years ago, and I know I've been going through this process for some time. I *have* found considerably more fulfillment. I met a guy who gave a sales pitch that was so elegant and concise, and it really gave me something to model after. Something I realized I was lacking along the way in building this business, is a mentor or a model to pattern my life after. My eyes are open now, and I'm better able to understand what I'm seeing. So much of my success is going on in my heart and in between my ears, rather than financially.

JOHN: So take us back a little bit about what it is that you're doing and how things have changed.

RICHARD: I still have a manufacturing firm. We manufacture a widget that is an after-market add-on in the air conditioning industry. It is a proprietary product that had no precedent when it was introduced to the market 20 years ago. I built it up and was deeply involved with the engineering and trying to do it all myself. But I had doubts about it. Not that it wouldn't be financially successful, but that I wouldn't be able to endure the tedium and all the other things you have to go through to get a business off the ground and through difficult times. I wasn't sure I had the mettle to persevere.

I brought in what some might call an executive coach. He's a friend of mine, so it's a lot deeper than executive coaching. He has nurtured me and kicked me in the ass when I needed it. He has given me a sounding board. Someone with perspective who can say, "Okay, now is the time. Let's add a couple of salespeople or do this or that."

He gets me to think through the challenges – because he doesn't know my industry, but he knows me. He knew that I could think through and determine what the right answer was, if I was patient enough. The way he labels it is "helping me get out of my own way." We all have certain personality traits that perhaps create obstacles that are impediments to our own success.

JOHN: In your earlier life, you had a considerable ebb and flow of success. It just didn't come easy. With some of our entrepreneurs it just seems to happen. It didn't seem like it happened easily for you. It seemed like you were struggling a lot.

RICHARD: True, but I think the fact that I was struggling a lot was because of my own issues. I was causing more problems for myself than the external environment was. It wasn't coming easy, but if I look back, it hasn't been hard. I have known the right things to do; it's just been hard work.

JOHN: We also went back and looked at how you were trying to build a business and you had to go and wait tables and had built a million-dollar business.

RICHARD: That is true, I did go through that, but that is what building a small business is. Now I'm at a point where I'm realizing it is a bigger business. The conversation I had with my CPA this week was that there is no reason I couldn't scale this $2.5 million business to $10 million pretty easily without having trouble in the market or getting in over my head. When we last talked, my business was a $1 million business, so you can see that we've grown significantly.

TIFFANI: Your business has grown from $1million to $2.5 million, so I am assuming your personal net worth has grown as well? Before you had gold and stocks. How have those investments changed, or have they?

RICHARD: They haven't. What happened is that I kind of put them in place and realized, I am safe there. Through the downturn

I heard people talk about their 401(k)s. I was oblivious to it, because I wasn't thinking about it at all. It was a tough year, but I bounced back pretty quickly. Through that year, I kept the core position. I still have some concerns with monetary policy and all of that. I have an interest in it, and I read about it, but I'm not as dedicated to keeping my eye on it as I was. In fact, I took a risk in that time frame to hire my salesmen.

A year after our interview, I hired the executive coach. He and I came to the conclusion we needed an outside salesperson, because I couldn't stay on the road. What a difference! I was going to go out of my mind if I stayed out on the road, and that probably came out in my interview with you.

Though I was having success, it was small in comparison to what I should have been having. I realized then that I have such a huge opportunity, and if I just follow through, within five years I could pretty much retire happily. Now, I have actually gotten to the point where I don't want to retire, because I don't have to do the BS I didn't enjoy anymore.

Have I had fabulous success beyond my wildest dreams?

I'm not there yet, but I have this vision of where I'm going.

When I talked to you last, my father had passed away a year earlier, and I was in mourning more than I realized. He had gotten me into this business, and I wanted to kill him for it, but I also want to hug him for it. I love it and I hate it.

I'll never be as good at anything else as I have gotten at being good in the HVAC business. There is an elegance to the sale and a certain art that I have talked about with my coach that is essential to me enjoying what I do. If I can sell with a little bit of artistry and poetry, then I will feel more fulfilled than just seeing an HVAC solution delivered as, "Here is this part, and that part you put together like this." I want some elegance. I want something more than that.

TIFFANI: Wow, I love that. Did you start saving a significant amount more during that time?

RICHARD: No, I put most of it back into the business. I don't have it stashed away, but the business is worth considerably more now. If I wanted to sell it today, I could get as much as $5 million for it. I'm not sure I want that. If I can increase it by four times, maybe I'll just keep it there to throw off cash, and I can do other things I want to do.

I have competent management in place that would allow me to do that. I have a sales team in place. We've built all the pieces, and now I have other people build them for me. So, to answer your question, my pile of cash isn't any bigger.

JOHN: The success is helping breed the contentment. Success makes you feel good.

RICHARD: It is satisfying in some ways. It isn't an end in itself, but I see the light at the end of the tunnel. Within five years, I could go away. I make a joke around the office that they are all working towards my retirement, when I'll be sitting on the beach drinking piña coladas. Or I'm going to move to Costa Rica and learn how to surf. It's always a couple of years away. It's something I've visualized for a long time, and now I am maybe close enough to make it happen, since I'm 50 years old. The satisfaction is implicit in the success I've had.

JOHN: It's interesting talking to entrepreneurs over the years. There is no easy path.

RICHARD: Exactly. There's no simple calculation or calculus for "it," except hard work, and you've just gotta keep showing up with the right approach.

I would also like to say, "fortune favors the prepared mind." I had a girlfriend at that time that said, "You are going to work with your father, *that* father, you are out of your mind." She was almost right. But I told her that I could foresee a path – though, if I knew it would be 20 years, I am not sure if I would have signed on, but I did see a path to controlling my life.

To be an entrepreneur you just keep showing up. I had the opportunity to control my own destiny and have independence on a scale I couldn't imagine.

JOHN: Where are you trying to go now? I bet you're having that conversation with yourself.

RICHARD: If you're not asking yourself that, then it's not good.
I'm learning as I go, and it's part of building an organization and a team. I think of them all as my family. As I find the right ones that fit in; I see them being a part of my long-term planning, no matter what that entails. I hope to be able to reward them for their loyalty, as they have been giving so much to me. I am trying to maintain the connections with people. Ultimately, it's not just about money.

What did you hear about money growing up?
The financial world is unproductive. Build something that will build real wealth. In the end Dad and I succeeded, together, though he rarely admitted it in my presence.

Most important life lesson
My father's failures in business. He thought he knew it all and constantly made mistakes by not seeking legal counsel or asking for help.

One thing you learned about life you would want to pass down to future generations
You cannot tell anyone anything. They have to be ready to listen.

Favorite books
Sometimes a Great Notion (Ken Kesey); *Zen and the Art of Motorcycle Maintenance* (Robert Pirsig); *The Redemption of Christopher Columbus* (Orson Scott Card); *Alexander Hamilton* (Ron Chernow); *The Road* (Cormac McCarthy); *Jitterbug Perfume* (Tom Robbins).

SIX *MORE* YEARS LATER ...
Net Worth Increased to $6 Million

One of our absolute favorite quotes from Richard six years ago was, "So much of my success is going on in my heart and in between my ears, rather than financially." This next encounter caught us up on how he has continued down the road of that journey.

This time, Richard started off letting us know that he couldn't imagine at all what he said previously, because he knows what he used to believe, and how things have changed. Cue our Indiana Jones curiosity waiting to hear the rest of the story.

Richard's business did grow, but not as substantially as he would have liked. They had some "interesting" interruptions. He found out that some of the employees were not acting in his best interest. Changes ensued. "We sort of started all over again, not to say that we lost a lot of momentum, but we didn't maintain the momentum. I had to bring in new people, and that is more of a challenge for customer continuity, at least in terms of how they deal with us and how the new people need to learn how to deal with them.

"It has required me to be more invested in the long run than I would have anticipated. I was not as able to delegate as I would have liked. Even though it didn't take me to the theoretical $10 million in volume, I feel like I did okay. The pandemic has been significant. We serve and sell to service companies like restaurants and malls and commercial systems. So we have had to change the way we approach the market. Where we were more service oriented, we now need to be more service-focused.

We had to interrupt here. In the last interview, he had said he was building a team and an organization that he had thought of as family and had a hope to reward them for their loyalty. What went wrong?

"Well, you hear about these things. Some of the key personnel were being duplicitous. We never found any absolute proof. And I didn't pursue it. We had enough information to understand that something was going on outside of our knowledge. There were a couple of customers that I was not comfortable dealing with; I could tell they were going to screw me in the long run. They're sort of out of business now, at least as far as I know. But I made choices about not continuing to work with them. And they represented a significant potential growth opportunity for us.

"I also felt a key salesman was doing some things without management approval and he was terminated, and some people left with him. That was pretty disappointing, but it happens.

"I hadn't been in the middle of it enough. I was sort of letting them have free rein, and in the process, I felt like things were going on that I uncovered later."

What is the process to recover from that? How do you rebuild the team and adjust to the change? In Richard's case, he just simply started talking to people. Getting to know them. This brought opportunities to have some conversations with people he ultimately wanted to hire. A couple of them ended up being key people.

"They might not have the same level of experience or depth of knowledge about the operation as I do, however, they possess the technical capabilities that I required the most. This is allowing me to take a more secure step back from daily operations. We also brought on a bunch of new guys who fit well in the team. They aren't quite as experienced either, but they will be fine."

And enter the pandemic. Richard had to get more involved, once again. He is unsure about the future. "I am prepared to jump back in; I have had my fingers in it. I wanted to watch and see what the economy and company were going to do. I am the only one who has been through it in this company before. I was in this business during 9/11 and the 2008 crisis. In some ways we still have opportunity. If a restaurant is operating at half capacity, they still require air conditioning.

"I don't feel like I am missing out on anything by not retiring at 55 and going to the beach with those piña coladas. It was an amusing way to describe where I hoped to be. But now, I have a much more interesting team and a much more interesting role. I am not dealing with the technical crap all the time. It is a significant relief. I am back into it in a deeper way, but I am also learning from it, so it has been positive in a lot of ways."

He has begun putting his energy into teaching more, guiding people so they understand how he goes about looking for opportunities that they don't get. It is a slow process. "I have to admit, I've sort of enjoyed teaching them some of these skill sets, and I've enjoyed watching them learn and grow. So, in some ways, it's been more rewarding to have this new team than the financial rewards of the other one and all the stress that came along with that.

"I have learned from this process as well. Just in terms of patience, I learned that I needed to have more patience, especially with kids in their twenties who are learning fast and have all sorts of ideas but need to be guided down the right path. I give them an example and show them what I do. 'Okay, here's this customer. He's called in; what do we know about him? What do we know about the customer he's selling to? What are they doing? You know, how are they doing it?' And so, I'm trying to teach them how to go through that process. Sometimes they are staring at me blankly, sometimes they are absorbing it, and as time goes on, they are getting better and better at it. I sort of enjoy watching them get better.

"And now, because of that, I can talk at a higher level with them, at a more theoretical level, which is really where I want to be talking about how to approach, you know, customer opportunities and sales. I mean, I'm a salesman at heart; you know, I was forced to be an engineer because there were no other engineers in my family, so I went to engineering school. But it wasn't something I wanted to pursue and didn't, but explaining and teaching that aspect of what I knew to the new kids, and even the older gentleman who works with me who knows a lot more about the specifics of air conditioning than I do, was beneficial.

"It's a pleasure to work with someone with whom I can have a high-level conversation. And then some of these young kids are building up to a point where they're starting to understand when I start rambling about, you know, my approach and how they should maybe take it or decide, you know, that I try to leave some space for them to figure out what works for them.

"My coach guides me through this process. I am learning what it is I like about what I do. So, what made me a good salesman is that all that I am doing is teaching people about what I have to offer and the benefit. I am teaching the team how to do that in a more consistent way than I used to do. I felt like it was such a risk when I was doing it, having to develop new talent. And now, the talent that is being developed is great, great talent, you know? I sometimes make a joke about how they are my audience too; you know I like to pay to get my audience."

Richard felt that leaving a place for them to figure it out was what his mentor did for him, how to give somebody the space so they can learn. Still giving them a framework to approach, but knowing how to step back and let them figure out some of the things that are going to work best for them.

Richard hadn't remembered in the last interview telling us that he had found a mentor and he felt that had been missing in his life, someone he wanted to model his life after. Now, he was coming full circle, with his staff. "I did realize that I couldn't pattern my life after this coach. I knew fairly soon after I probably made that statement. But I realized, he can help me figure out how to pattern my life for myself."

So, let's do the numbers. Six years ago, he wasn't saving and putting most back into the business. He was deciding whether he was going to try to put more away. Richard actually ended up adding another three-quarters of a million to his savings, and because of that has a different mix of investments.

"I have worked really hard to save in the last few years. Business was good, and I am continuing to put a lot more away than I was. Back then a large portion of my savings was gold, now it is a considerably smaller portion. I have simply broadened my horizons. I am glad I bought the gold when I did. When am I going to sell it? Who the hell knows? I am not that worried about it. I am fortunate to be in the position where I don't need it right now. I can continue to work and continue to save towards retirement."

Incredibly, even with the disruptions in business, he is taking more time for himself, writing and reading. A large portion is doing work on himself, time for reflection.

"I feel like it is paying off, because I have a better balance in my life right now. I just write for myself. I do a lot of that. It is kind of like thinking about looking inside my belly button and discovering what is inside might be worth something. I am spending time with friends, trying to increase my social circle. When I was talking last to you, I was in a relationship. It was a good relationship, and then it wasn't a good relationship. I learned a whole lot. Basically, ****!, how do I not do that again?

"One such reflection is I am learning to set better boundaries in my organization; some people require a lot of effort to manage. Dealing with that takes me away from what I do best."

John relayed a story of one of his own early mentors telling him about the "faucet principle." Basically, we are all faucets. If you let someone into your life and let them turn the faucet on, they can drain you of all you had. You want to give access to someone who will not abuse the faucet. They will take what you want them to take, walk away, and not leave it open. "John, that's it. That is brilliant. The issue is ensuring that you understand that just because you were told you couldn't set boundaries, did you end up letting too many of them drain the faucet. This is where I am trying to balance my life."

We couldn't help but let him know there has been a consistency in these third interviews. The statement that finances are less important, and they should focus more on themselves and their relationships. This has not been related to any specific age, it comes from those younger to those in their late seventies.

"Well, here's the deal for you to know: Much of my youth was 'misspent,' as others would often refer to my alcohol and drug abuse. I realized that I used a lot of that as insulation against the abuse of the people in my life. I have learned so much about myself, but I don't know how to express it. I tried to describe it to somebody I knew well. I am just becoming, you know, what I am becoming. Something other than I was, and I am okay with that. It means I am learning how to do it and getting better at it. You have to make a choice.

"The related question is whether or not you are ever really finished. It is a process, the amount of work that goes into becoming whatever you are going to become next. I am finding more rewards in the process than I ever found in making the money."

QUESTIONS FROM OUR OTHER MILLIONAIRES

What is important to you and how has that changed over time?
Now that my finances are covered and I don't have to worry about them in the future, I'm not worried about them at all. Whereas I used to be more actively involved in making sure that they were just right, or that they were going to be, and that I was putting enough money away and all that, I don't have that concern any longer. And I'm comfortable with continuing to work 24 hours a week, and what I do with the rest of my time is trying to figure out what else I'm going to do with that time, because I'm not a golfer, you know, that kind of thing.

What do you do in your spare time?
I am a bit of a painter and artist. I do a lot of walking around town. I enjoy writing; I write for myself. I am tempted to write something different, not more reflection, but maybe self-help. It will probably be a story of some sort.

Do you think you are rich?
Yes, absolutely. Yes, I am rich. I am not as wealthy or have as many friends as I once had. But I feel like I am richer, and my friends are higher quality. It's like having a dinner. I will have just five friends that have a deeper, more meaningful connection, and I appreciate what they are talking about vs. 50, who are less able to understand what I am talking about or communicate with that connection.

Quotes to Ruminate On

ADVICE MILLIONAIRES TOOK TO HEART

⚷ "Father's advice: Do what you love, and the money will take care of itself." —Scott

⚷ "Learn as much as possible – generally by reading." —William

⚷ "Never give up. Try again when you fail. Get the best deal possible on everything you buy. These ideas were learned at my father's knee." —Ray

⚷ "Be honest, have integrity, be true to your word, work hard, do what is necessary, even it is hot, cold, dirty, or otherwise unpleasant." —Richard

⚷ "I had several pivotal moments that I thought the world was just giving me lemons. One specifically: My mother and I were in an accident which resulted in her death. I realized that if I was going to be successful, I was going to have to accept challenges and make the best of what I was given. Essentially, I couldn't change the circumstances, but I could change my response to them." —Tracie

⚷ "I would say that number one on the list is just hard work. My parents were great role models for me, both in the workplace; both worked, and in the home. I was surrounded by people who had to really work very hard to make a living and that was something you embraced, not something you fought. I took that example to heart and believed life was always about work." —Jacki

CHAPTER 5

From Immigrant to the American Dream Embodied

GEORGE D.
Net Worth: $6 Million
Income: $150–200k
Started Investing: 27
Attained Millionaire Status: 41

Coming to America at the age of 9, George was placed on a new path for his life by the generations that came before.

Being Greek immigrants in Turkey had not been a good thing, George recounts, so his family finally left after the Turkish government tried to tax his father's business 90%. "I remember we left shortly after my ninth birthday – they seemed to think that was important, so we did. I was in fourth grade, and my father's brother had been in the United States so we came as well. My mother's side of the family ended up in Australia. Being a Greek in Turkey, just like being a Turk in Greece, those things were not good. They were not conducive to making money and seeing it. I have since learned that my father had a travel agency and a trading business in the Middle East, mostly in Lebanon, Greece, and Iraq. They had a Turkish partner as a figurehead and the government figured it out and started taxing them at 90%. That was their way of saying, 'We don't really want you to stay.'"

When they came to the United States, no one in the family spoke English; this was just the first obstacle they met with resilience to thrive. George's father was a tailor, eventually became the head fitter at

Brooks Brothers, and began investing in real estate. Even as his father became successful, he was always frugal, taking his sandwiches and soft drinks to work each day.

"Back then I think vending machines were 25 cents. He thought buying a soft drink from a vending machine at lunch was a waste of money. He always said to guard your money very, very carefully. Don't waste it. If you're going to buy cars, drive as hard a bargain as humanly possible. When you go stay at a hotel, look to get the best deal. He and one of his friends would be planning a vacation – two Greek men, they were constitutionally incapable of paying retail. They were always negotiating with hotels, and they would call from place to place to get a better deal.

"It was a wrenching experience coming from a country where we had roots for generations. We certainly never felt poor, but we were lower-middle-class. We never really went without. He taught me the value of hard work and the value of saving. Even to this day he holds onto his cars 8, 10, 12 years.

"None of us spoke any English when we came here. In foreign schools we start to learn a foreign language. In primary school in Istanbul it was French, because my mother had some French blood in her. If they had to do it all over again, I am sure they would have started me in English."

Even though his father did not speak English, he always had a skill to fall back on. There were always opportunities for advancement for someone who was a craftsman or had a certain skill. He pounded into George's head the importance of saving for a rainy day.

The patriarch of the family was not the only one who worked hard for his success: George did well in school and went to college and then on to law school. When he looks back on his education, he says he was the embodiment of the American Dream.

"I was taught, the line from Polonius in Hamlet – 'neither a borrower nor a lender be.' My father didn't want me to take out any student loans, but we didn't have a single extra penny. Even so, my father paid for the majority of my education, and I paid for the rest by working at a grocery store and as a researcher at the US Patent Office. So, there was not a single solitary penny of student loans.

"I had started out working for a large firm in New York where they encouraged specialization, so they sent me to NYU. They forced me to go to NYU to get a master's in tax law." In law school, even though George specialized in tax law, he moved into business planning and business analysis and eventually into internet law. "After moving to a smaller boutique firm, instead of just giving tax advice, one was expected to draft one's own documents, to be familiar with corporate law, so I made a gradual transition to business analysis. From there it wasn't much of a leap to go into internet law. One of my mentors was egging me – pushing me in the direction of writing a book. My law school roommate and I wrote a book on the internet and law; we ended up with some clients, and lo and behold, I ended up in internet law."

It wasn't until after he began practicing law and was making a good salary, that he started saving about 25% of his annual income. "For the first two to three years I lived in New York and was a bachelor. There were infinite ways you could spend money in search of a better party. The last two years a light bulb went on and I started putting money in my IRA and in the bank. It was very straightforward; out of every deposited check I took 25% of it and put it in a separate savings account."

Although he does not currently save that much, in his opinion, he still manages to put aside around 12% a year. "I think a more fundamental reason why I'm not saving the same right now is when I had a steady paycheck every two weeks, money would magically appear in my bank account by direct deposit and would be the same amount. Now that I am a business owner, my checks are more irregular. I have a few clients that are on retainer, so I know I am going to be paid quarterly by them. The rest of the time, I may get paid by five or six clients one month and receive nothing the next month."

He shared that most of his money is in stocks. "I can tell you, even though I read your newsletter and knew in my bones what was coming the past two years, I didn't sell as many stocks as I should have when it was time. I sold some. I started out the year with $2.3 million in stocks and those are now worth $1.9 million in the last two and half months. I admit I even have some mutual funds. I don't like mutual funds much; I think they are grossly inefficient, so I invest my own money."

We got curious as to why he would stay in, when he was telling himself the market is going down. "I can probably give it to you with one good example rather than try to analyze it. I remember the day. I was vacationing in Florida. It was a Monday. That was the day that

Goldcorp hit its 52-week high of 52 bucks and change. I had bought the darn thing at 21 and I think I injured myself from patting myself on the back for being such a genius. I didn't want to pay the long-term capital gain. I could see the way the government acted; it was in your newsletters, there for anyone that wanted to see it. But I didn't want to pay the capital gains on 30 bucks a share. If that isn't the height of stupidity, I don't know what is. Twenty percent between Virginia and the Feds would have let me keep 24. As it turns out it is now more or less where I bought it. Especially, as a tax lawyer, I don't know how many times I have told clients to not let the tax tail wag the dog, yet that is exactly what I did. The joke now is I didn't want to pay capital gains taxes, and therefore I don't have to worry anymore about paying capital gains taxes."

He gets most of his investment information from the internet, Value Line, *Thoughts from the Frontline*, and Morningstar. "I look through things that people point out, and then I go do my own due diligence. I spend a few days gathering as much research as I can about a company, and then I buy it myself. Even though I don't want to make a habit of losing, I believe you learn more from your losses than you ever do from your wins. I find the companies that look to me like they are in a potential turnaround situation, don't have a huge amount of debt, can fix their problems and turn themselves around." He has about $2.3 million in the market with about $2 million in stocks and a small amount in mutual funds. Interestingly, he does not own more than 20 stocks in total, in fairly concentrated positions.

"I am a little more aggressive than my father. He is very, very conservative. He made his money in real estate. Like many other folks who do not have facility with the native tongue, he was able to invest in businesses that didn't require any great social skill or great access to the language. If you buy your real estate in a decent location and you're comfortable with the cash flow, you don't have to speak the language. Still though, my brother and I both get our habits of hard work, saving for a rainy day, and doing due diligence before you invest, from him.

"I've done some estate planning as favors to friends. A lot of Greeks and Italians who are worth anywhere from $5–30 million, it is all real estate. They bought mini-malls, strip centers, etc., in areas that looked like they were going to improve before they improved.

"One of the most valuable lessons I have learned along the way is from a gentleman who was a scout in World War II in Patton's army. It was this: If you're going from Point A to Point B, the fact that you may be in Area C is what matters. The fact that you were in Point A two hours ago is no longer relevant. He would look at stocks and investments and his business this way. He wasn't interested in how much money he spent on the business. He wasn't interested in what he paid for a stock. He wanted to know at any given point if he would buy more of the stock; would he be investing more in the business; did it make sense for the future? Never mind about the past. Never mind how you got to where you got. If you buy a stock at $15, and it is now $12, you need to decide whether it remains a good buy at that price. The fact that you paid $15 does not matter."

Although George has lived a successful life, when pressed about if he would retire, he is just not ready. "It's not appreciably different from what you wrote yourself, John. I'd like to be able to do what interests me for as long as I can. I don't want to be working every day in an office, but I would like to do what interests me as long as I am physically and mentally able to do it. I do want to be able to have more control over my schedule. I don't ever really want to retire and just do nothing."

George has young daughters and has often thought about the daunting task of how to talk to them about the economic world. "I live in an affluent area. The kids at their elementary school have absolutely no concept of money. They think that money grows on trees. To give you an example: My daughter asked me when she was nine if we were going to Vail or Cancun for spring break. The kids in her class were all going somewhere, and she asked why we were not. I do try to tell them that not everyone lives like this. That really, no more than one or two people out of a hundred can do what others in her class do and they take it for granted. She wasn't lobbying for a vacation, she just thought, 'It is spring break, doesn't everyone go somewhere for spring break?' With my parents there were limits. We knew we could only get a certain number of things. We were not entitled to a lot of vacation time. If we got to spend one or two weeks at local beaches a year, that was a treat, but my daughters think that going to Australia is etched in stone. Teaching them about money is going to be hard."

At the time of this interview, we were entering the Great Recession, but George wasn't worried. In fact, true to his father's refusal to ever pay retail, you could almost say he was a little eager for it.

"I want my children to understand that a recession is normal, and not to fear it. If you save enough money, recessions can give you the opportunity to improve your lot. I bought my house during a recession. A recession gives you the opportunity to buy something for a significant discount. It is also perfectly normal because people get excited, they go to excess, and we have to hit the reset button. I want my daughters to understand that this is just normal. It is not to be feared or loved, just accepted."

George beamed about a closely held company he is associated with and the uniqueness of its growth. In his own words: "It is one of the happiest things I am associated with. It is a video production company called Acorn Media Group. I had met a man through a friend and he needed someone to do some legal work because he was trying to get a company started and raise a bit of money to produce two or three videos. One of them was called 'Virginia Plantations,' another called 'Washington Monument.' I helped him with fundraising, and he raised $40,000 and was able to piece together two videos. In fact, I still have one of the originals back from 1987. From that company that started in the basement of his house, the company's revenues this year are going to hit quite big this year [George asked us to keep this number confidential].

"It really is just a fun company. It licenses and distributes quite a bit of Anglophile videos like *Foyle's War*, *Prime Suspect*, and *Hercule Poirot*. Essentially, a *Masterpiece Theater*–like model. He has two catalogs. One is a health and wellness line called Acacia that is newer. It has Bollywood dance, yoga, mind-body-spirit, a bit of music. He also has his media catalog. The model is he pays dividend distributions to cover our tax liability and depending on the availability of cash in the company he will make others, when cash is burning a hole in his pocket. Sometimes the cash stays in to pay royalty advances and sublicense products. It really is an all-American success story."

Family is everything to George, and he enjoys traveling with his kids to other parts of the world, as he wants to broaden their minds. "I believe meeting others is the best way to overcome prejudice." He believes strongly that you are only as good as your friends and family and that they are the key to a happy life. Finally, he believes strongly in giving back. George says that God put us on this earth to help those less fortunate than ourselves. To him, this is a categorical imperative.

A fun side note into George's outlook on life. In our interview, we were disconnected briefly. When we came back on, George commented, "It is kind of funny. I was going to hang up, but then the music they were playing was Louis Armstrong. I figured you can't go too far wrong by waiting for the end of a good song."

SIX YEARS LATER ...
Net Worth Increased to $7.5 Million

TIFFANI: When we last talked, you were financially pretty conservative. Most of your money was still in stocks, and you said you wanted to tell your children that recessions are an opportunity to improve your lot. Did you take advantage of the recession that hit?

GEORGE: I think I may end up being odd, because I actually made a ton of money in 2008 and 2009. Mostly because I was short a bunch of the subprime lenders. I was short the garbage companies that I knew would no longer exist, like Countrywide and Century Financial.

JOHN: Was that because you were in the affordable housing area, and you could see what was happening?

GEORGE: Well, it was two things. One of them was you. What you had been writing since 2005 reinforced what I was thinking. Then another thing that kicked it in was that one of my friends owned an auto body shop. In 2007 he called me and said that two of his body shop employees had asked if he would loan them $10,000 and they would repay him $10,500 the following Monday. He thought that was really odd and asked why they needed it. They said that they were buying houses and the mortgage broker said they needed an extra $10,000 in the bank on Friday, but by Monday no one would care where it went. Then he asked his book-keeper if they had gotten any calls confirming employment or salary, and the bookkeeper said no. I knew who they were and how much they made, and these guys were buying $600,000 houses and were making $50,000 on them. That just doesn't compute. So, then I decided to start shorting some of the subprime lenders. These subprime guys were doing next to nothing and then decided to diversify – or to 'de-worsify.' Around that time, you were writing letters, scratching your head saying, wait, how can they slice and dice something that is subprime and then have a portion of it be AAA-rated? It doesn't make sense. That doesn't work. So, it was a bunch of things that came together. I bought leaps, either a year and a half or two and a half years out of the money.

JOHN: So, you were just raking in money. Not only were you shorting, but you were also leveraging your shorts.

GEORGE: Exactly. I think I had the January 2009 Countrywide 35 or 37½ *puts* [a type of option that increases in value as a stock falls]. I was short a couple thousand shares, but more importantly I was up by 20 or 30 *leaps* [options that have expiration dates of at least 12 months into the future]. I did that to First Union, NBIA, Countrywide. It was like shoot-ing fish in a barrel. I was seeing the market. I was seeing what was going on around me. Then I was reading people like you. It was either a virtuous cycle or a vicious cycle, because the people who were doing thoughtful analysis were all saying the same thing. And 90% of the country was on the other side. So that worked out pretty well. My mistake over the last few years was mostly being out of the market, because I don't believe in it. I think it is heavily manipulated. I don't think it's organic market growth. I think it's Fed-fueled. But then saying that, what did I miss? A 100% gain or whatever it was.

TIFFANI: Where are most of your investments right now?

GEORGE: My investments are mostly in the stock market. I have about a quarter of my investments – or rather, I think of it as insurance – in gold.

TIFFANI: So actual gold or gold stocks?

GEORGE: Not stocks. It used to be a segregated account. I should be more aware of how my gold is being held. Yes, there is a delivery, but I would say that there are maybe a hundred of us who have a claim to a particular side of the warehouse; but if something really goes wrong, I'm not sure all of us get delivery. It's certainly not a *pooled account* [like a mutual fund or exchange-traded fund]. Those are nonstarters for me.

TIFFANI: So, you are a little diversified. Part of your net worth is in stocks; some is in gold. Where are you getting your income?

GEORGE: What income? The Treasury bonds don't pay interest; it's just a coupon strip, so the interest is imputed, and it's more a trading vehicle. I have some two-year Treasuries. The only income of any consequence I'm getting is that I own what used to be known as Bell Atlantic, which is now Verizon. I have owned some of these stocks forever. Exxon and Chevron. The forever stocks I own, the ones that I have owned 10 years or longer, are paying me halfway decent dividends. But I can't find any decent source of interest income without taking exorbitant risk, and I'm not willing to do that.

When I say I'm out of the stock market, there are some stocks I have that are forever. Those stocks I don't really ever intend to touch. I bought them anywhere from 1987 to 2001, and those are my trading vehicles. I don't really consider them as anything other than something sitting there and paying me dividends and hopefully appreciating in price.

As far as actual stocks, I intend to be in the gold miners soon, but I am not now. I have a bunch of cash sitting on the sidelines collecting 25 *basis points* [basis points or "bips" are 1/100 of a percent – 25 basis points is .25%], and I'm waiting for an opportunity to invest. I think the next step might be to buy a couple of houses to generate income.

One thing that has nothing to do with the credit crunch since the first time we talked is I invested in one of my clients, and my client got sold. I got a large chunk of money. That is why I pick and choose my assignments. It had nothing to do with my genius in these markets, it was just fortuitous.

JOHN: Well, I would say it wasn't just fortuitous that you invested with your friend. It was good judgment and the due diligence you referred to previously.

GEORGE: I tend to view it more as luck being the residue of good planning. I have provided legal services for next to nothing for people I knew or liked. I did it for six entities. Four of them never amounted to anything. One of them was a company that drilled for oil and did spectacularly well. It was a small amount of money, but the rate of return for me was phenomenal. And then there was Acorn Media that got acquired. Those were the big hits. If you invest in half a dozen and get one or two hits, you are lucky.

JOHN: What is your net worth now?

GEORGE: Including my houses, $8–9 million. Excluding them, $7.5 million. I don't tend to count my house, because a house is something you live in, not something that generates a great deal of value. You hope that it will over 20–30 years, but it doesn't change my lifestyle one iota.

TIFFANI: So, you are sitting on all this cash, and you are looking for an opportunity. If this was your dream world, where would you be putting your money right now?

GEORGE: I am starting to become more European in my asset allocation. I want some hard assets that, even if not they're not beyond the reach of the government, are at least assets that generate some cash or provide some insurance that the government can't easily manipulate. I am waiting for the next recession, and I would like to buy another house or two. I think I would like to buy a vacation house in Southern California. Otherwise, I would like to buy another house for monthly income. The smartest thing my father did was buy two rental properties, which are free and clear and generate $6,000 each month come hell or high water. They haven't needed much in the way of repairs, because he did a fair amount of work on them a few years ago. He is all set. No matter what happens to anything else, he can pretty much count on $72,000 rolling in. He has no debt or expenses. He and my mom live just fine. I want hard assets. The other thing I want is more gold. I want something that the government can't print more of.

TIFFANI: We didn't talk much about your kids in the previous interview. You did say you hadn't talked to them too much about money. Now that they're older, have you had more money conversations?

GEORGE: My daughter would have been about 10 and my youngest daughter 7 then. It's interesting seeing how they've developed. My youngest daughter is a saver and a world-class miser. If she can get her mother or me to pay for something she wants, fine. Otherwise, she'll save for it. She doesn't spend.

The older one, Mara, is a little freer with her money. Mara worked for the first time this summer, as a lifeguard. She was able to make a couple thousand dollars. I told her, the most important thing is that whenever you make money, pay yourself first. Somewhere between 10 and 20% needs to go into a rainy-day account or retirement account or something. Something that gives you a cushion so that if hard times ever hit, you have money. If hard times never hit, then keep right on saving for your retirement. She is beginning to get it.

My youngest daughter, Kayla, who is now 13, doesn't quite understand those concepts. However, she doesn't spend. She is one of those kids who thinks she should spend less and save. When she wants something, she tries to make sure someone else buys it for her so she can keep her money. When her piggy bank ever begins to get low, she starts grumbling and looking for ways to make money.

One of the things we do is to have the girls run a neighborhood dog-walking and dog-sitting service. We have elderly people who live in our area, and they go away for a couple of weeks at a time. They used to board their dogs. They are very happy to have Kayla do it – though a lot of time we walk the dog – rather than have it boarded. She also does some babysitting that helps replenish that piggy bank.

The next step will be for me to talk to them about investments. My oldest daughter has now become socially conscious – to say it delicately. She doesn't like that I invest in oil. In a way, it kind of makes me think, and the conclusion I've come up with is that unless you invest in a company that is beyond the pale, everything is fair game. Make your money, and if you want to contribute to your local charities or give to your local homeless shelter, you should. I encourage that, and I think it's important to do.

We talk about community service a lot. I tell them, if you make money, set aside a little bit for the local food bank or a battered women's shelter. I also encourage them to volunteer. I want to teach them to be engaged in the community. I want them to be charitably inclined. I want them to appreciate how lucky we have been. We could be stuck in Turkey or some other place with turmoil and no opportunity for advancement. I think that is important for them to appreciate.

One thing that does concern me is they really don't understand the concept of not having enough. I hope they don't ever have to understand that concept, but currently they don't get it at all.

George commented that the stupidest things he ever spent money on was a lousy, unprofessional repair job of his driveway and Commodore Computer stock. "The driveway showed me the perils of failing to do due diligence. The shares of Commodore Computers are high on my list. It shows the perils of buying into a company with a failing product and a stubborn management that will not adapt." George added that some items are definitely worth the money, such as a well-cut men's suit and fine wine – preferably a red burgundy which he so generously sent us a few bottles.

He left us with the most important thing he has learned about life that he would want to be passed down to future generations. "You are only as good as your friends and family. God put you on this earth to help those less fortunate than you. It is the categorical imperative."

What did you hear about money growing up?
Individuals, like nations, should not spend more than they earn. You should always save for a rainy day and your family's future.

What personal character trait do you attribute to your success?
My willingness to take advice from others and to do my own research. I will not buy a stock or fund without understanding its business, as best I can. If I do not understand the business or balance sheet, I will not buy the stock. With mutual funds, I have to be comfortable with the investment style.

Greatest threat to individuals' wealth accumulation
Ignorance and laziness. As Peter Lynch has said, people spend hours trying to figure out which appliance to buy, but they are content to buy stocks or mutual funds on someone else's recommendation, without doing their own due diligence and research.

Favorite books
Moby Dick; *The Iliad*; *The Odyssey*; *Sentimental Education* (Flaubert); *The Red and the Black* (Stendahl); *Adventures of Huckleberry Finn* and other moldy-oldies. I also enjoy Peter Bernstein's book on the history of risk and Nassim Taleb's books.

SIX *MORE* YEARS LATER ...
Net Worth Increased to $9 Million

We jump back in with George feeling he hasn't made as much money in the last six years as he could have or should have. He spent money on things that "fill them up," which he is philosophically opposed to, but so be it. He spent eight years of tuition money on private schools for his daughters (The next comment was John Mauldin's trademark "sigh" here, seven kids and private schools later, he feels that deeply).

Now, they are both in college. That has made a difference in his cash flow. On the other hand, he does feel blessed. One of his points he made to himself, "What else are you going to spend money on?" He ended up taking that out of a brokerage account. If you're curious, the four years of private high school cost $340,000.

He now works only about 15 hours a week. He has helped a lot of people with their businesses getting loans, sorting unemployment benefits, and filing unemployment appeals when the powers that be cut someone off. As you can imagine, none of those people are in a position to pay much, if anything.

"What I ended up doing was working pro bono. I just had to decide whether I liked the person or the business enough, that is really what it comes down to. In the last five or six months I have made around $20,000. I am working more but making a whole lot less. Otherwise, my finances are in good shape."

In catching up about his daughters, he had a desire to have them meet people outside of the expensive private schools and was beginning to teach them about market cycles and that recession is normal. They were much younger then. But we wanted to know what his game plan is now.

"Let me start with a tiny little anecdote from last Saturday. One of my daughters is in college; she's at Oberlin. And while their school has opened [this was late 2020], not everyone is present. It's a hybrid model. Some people are online, and some people are there in person. And she was complaining about a couple of things. And I finally told her, 'You know, honey, these are rich white girls' problems.' Stop bitching about them. 'But, I am a rich white girl?' she said without pausing. Sigh.

"So, what am I teaching them? That's a really good question. I'm currently attempting to teach them that there are a lot of people who are struggling and suffering, and we should not take anything for granted. And as far as investments go, I tell them that paper assets are fine; hard assets are even better. That's what I've been trying to communicate to them the last few years: You're going to want to own hard assets, whether it's real estate, gold, or God knows what else you're going to want to own as hard assets. Well, are you?"

And … to the numbers. George's net worth has increased to about $9 million without his primary house. His portfolio comprises three houses he rents out jointly with his brother, stock positions (the largest are with United and American Airlines) and all the rest is in gold and gold stocks. He is up about 50%.

"I do well in a crappy market. My father taught me that the worse the market, the better. After his experience in Turkey and the lira fluctuations, his father learned a lesson. He told me, 'I am not going to have this happen again. I need some assets that will retain their value, that can't be printed, that can't be debased.' I inherited my father's gold, which he started buying at $350 an ounce. I haven't sold any of it."

Income-wise, he lives off his rental income, dividend income, wife's salary, and the money from his legal profession. Rental income brings in about $45,000, $40,000 in dividends, $20,000 from his legal profession, and his wife's income.

George has a trust set up with the two kids. It is comprised mostly of the company they ended up selling, Acorn Media Group. They eventually got acquired by the movie channel AMC paying annual dividends with an S corporation. Although technically not taxable, dividends were paid to cover each shareholder's tax liability. So, George then put some of the stock in a trust for his daughters and gave them some of his. They ended up with a decent-sized trust when the company was sold, although they barely know that exists and no one is about to tell them. (He did not tell us to keep this off the record – although we have purposely left out the number.)

Fun side note that screamed tongue-in-cheek, "Millionaires, they are just like us." George was confessing he had lost John's contact information. "Let's just say I learned paper doesn't crash. It also does not short-circuit when submerged in water. So, I was bending over, trying to jiggle something with the toilet when I realized I had the phone in my short's pocket. I bent over and, well there you have it."

QUESTIONS FROM OUR OTHER MILLIONAIRES

Do you think you are rich?
I guess I am. That is based solely on a statistical analysis of the top 5–10%. I understand where I belong, because I can look at the tables.

The answer to the question, "Do you feel wealthy?" My father used to say, "You're never really rich. If it can vanish, you never really feel richer, safer, or more secure." If you remember the first 30–40 years, you don't feel rich. For me, richness is justified by the question, "Can I have everything I want?" And as long as I can have most of what I want, I think that's rich enough for me. That's all it comes down to. It doesn't come down to "so and so has more" or "so and so has less." It comes down to "What are my own little needs?" Can I provide for my family? Can my kids go to college? And I have some money left over. And if that's the case, I feel rich.

What is important to you and how has that changed over time?
I don't know if it has changed over time, but I found that what is important to me is to share and spend time with my family. I always used to think of the Willie Nelson line: "Money is like manure." It is not good unless you spread it around. To me, that matters, it just does. Whether that means I spend time helping people or whether that means I donate some, I do those things.

The one thing my mother's dementia has taught me is how important it is to have people visiting the dementia ward, because I know in the dementia ward of that nursing home, there are 28 residents, and I would say a good half of them might get one visit a month if that. I try to be able to visit two or three other people there just because, you know, everyone wants to see someone. No one should have to be alone.

Were there any significant turning points in your life, in hindsight?
There are two possibilities. One would have been leaving New York and coming back to the DC area, where my parents lived, and

(continued)

ending up with a chance encounter with someone who was looking for legal work. And that is how Acorn Media came to be. That was worth a few million bucks later on.

The other turning point would have been the one that I might have mentioned before. In 1994, my law firm misrepresented things to me, which is not the first time; you'd be shocked. They didn't make any of us partners. And then they said, "We'll revisit this in a few months." There was nothing to revisit; I just asked him to buy me out, because I knew sooner or later, I was going to be told, "Don't darken our offices."

That turned out to be a blessing in disguise because I was much happier as a sole proprietor and a sole practitioner with just a small law firm affiliation over the next 25 years. So, you can pick either of those as turning points. One was meeting my friend, Pete, and the other would have been being told you're not going to make partner and there isn't a future for you here.

How do you make important decisions?
I learned years ago that there is a fundamental difference between me and my beloved – my wife believes that things have a cause and effect. I don't. Sometimes they can, but it just doesn't work out that way. I don't believe in diversity; my investments are not diverse. I never had an overwhelming desire to own 20 to 30 stocks, or a bunch of bonds, or bunch of this and that. So, I get investment advice from people who mention something to me, then I dive down and figure out whether it makes sense combined from things I already know.

How do I make broader decisions? I have a bad temper, which I have been working on. It is getting better. What I have never done, when it comes to personal or financial decisions, is act irrationally. I try to take a day or two; sometimes I will take out a yellow notebook. I'll write the pros on one side and the cons on the other, trying to figure out what I should do. As a result, I try to take my time and not rush into anything. And then I learned one thing from having a Greek father who was in all sorts of businesses: I never pay retail. I just don't know; everything can be negotiated.

Charts

**HOW MUCH IS YOUR MOTIVATION TO
ACCUMULATE WEALTH RUN BY FEAR AND LACK
OF SECURITY?**

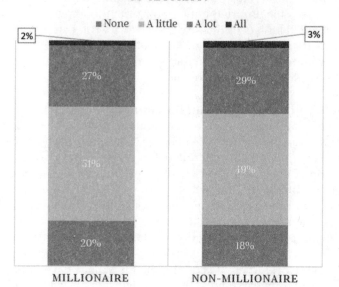

DO YOU BELIEVE YOU WILL RECEIVE AN INHERITANCE IN THE FUTURE?

■ No ■ Yes

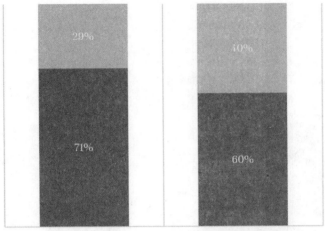

MILLIONAIRE   NON-MILLIONAIRES

HOW IMPORTANT IS MONEY TO YOUR PERSONAL HAPPINESS?

■ Not Important   ■ Somewhat Important   ■ Very Important

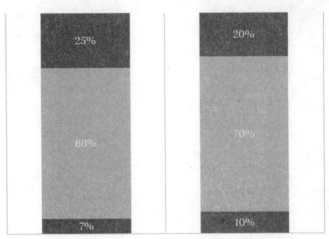

MILLIONAIRE   NON-MILLIONAIRE

DO YOU FEEL YOUR PATTERNS OF MONEY AND FINANCE ARE THE
SAME AS YOUR PARENTS?

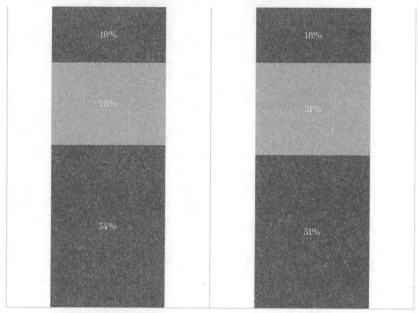

DO YOU FEEL YOUR PATTERNS OF MONEY AND FINANCE ARE THE SAME AS YOUR PARENTS?

■ No   ■ Somewhat   ■ Yes

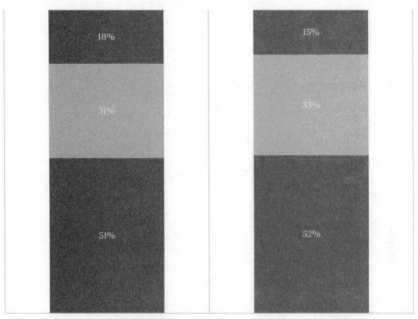

NON-MILLIONAIRES 2008   NON-MILLIONAIRE 2023

WHERE DO YOU GET YOUR FINANCIAL ADVICE AND INFORMATION TO FIND OPPORTUNITIES?

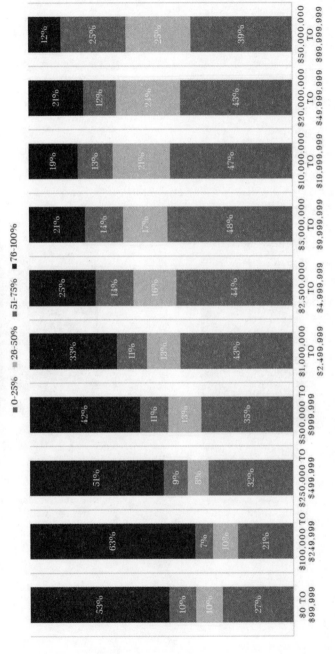

WHAT PERCENTAGE OF YOUR INCOME IS "ACTIVE" VS "PASSIVE" (YOUR MONEY OR BUSINESS STREAM IS WORKING FOR YOU)?

■ 0-25%   ■ 26-50%   ■ 51-75%   ■ 76-100%

	$0 TO $99,999	$100,000 TO $249,999	$250,000 TO $499,999	$500,000 TO $999,999	$1,000,000 TO $2,499,999	$2,500,000 TO $4,999,999	$5,000,000 TO $9,999,999	$10,000,000 TO $19,999,999	$20,000,000 TO $49,999,999	$50,000,000 TO $99,999,999
0-25%	53%	63%	51%	42%	33%	25%	21%	19%	21%	12%
26-50%	10%	7%	9%	11%	11%	14%	14%	13%	12%	25%
51-75%	10%	10%	8%	13%	13%	16%	17%	21%	24%	25%
76-100%	27%	21%	32%	35%	43%	44%	48%	47%	43%	39%

HOW CONCERNED ARE YOU ABOUT MAINTAINING YOUR
CURRENT FINANCIAL CONDITION?

■ What? Me worry?   ■ Not Concerned   ■ Comfortable
■ Somewhat Concerned   ■ Extremely Concerned

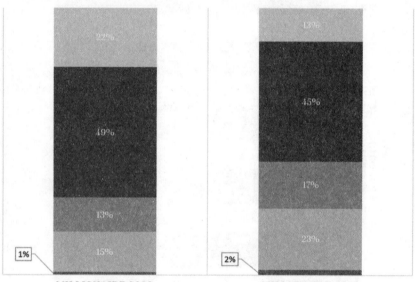

MILLIONAIRE 2008   MILLIONAIRE 2023

HOW CONCERNED ARE YOU ABOUT MAINTAINING YOUR CURRENT FINANCIAL CONDITION?

■ What? Me worry?   ■ Not Concerned   ■ Comfortable
■ Somewhat Concerned   ■ Extremely Concerned

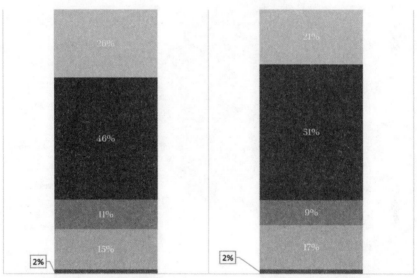

NON-MILLIONAIRE 2008   NON-MILLIONAIRE 2023

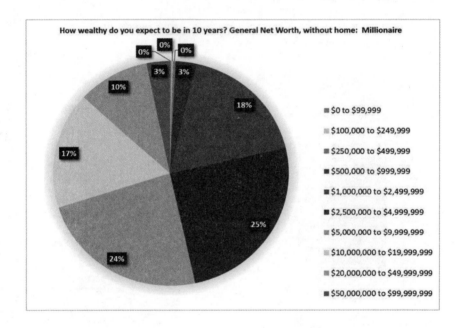

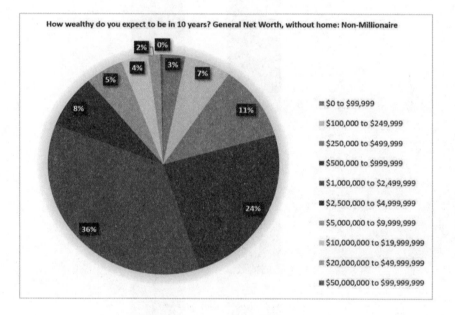

How wealthy do you expect to be in 10 years? General Net Worth, without home: Non-Millionaire

- $0 to $99,999
- $100,000 to $249,999
- $250,000 to $499,999
- $500,000 to $999,999
- $1,000,000 to $2,499,999
- $2,500,000 to $4,999,999
- $5,000,000 to $9,999,999
- $10,000,000 to $19,999,999
- $20,000,000 to $49,999,999
- $50,000,000 to $99,999,999

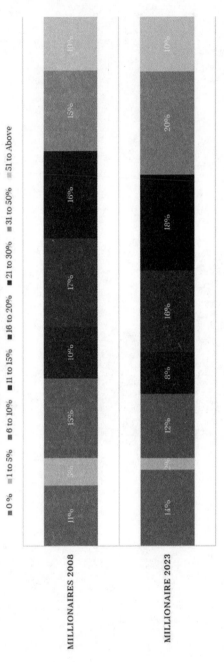

WHAT PERCENTAGE OF YOUR HOUSEHOLD INCOME DO YOU SAVE/INVEST A YEAR FOR LONG-TERM PURPOSES? (IE: EDUCATION, RETIREMENT, ETC.)

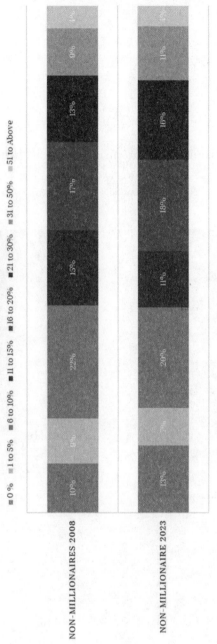

WHAT PERCENTAGE OF YOUR HOUSEHOLD INCOME DO YOU SAVE/INVEST A YEAR FOR LONG-TERM PURPOSES? (IE: EDUCATION, RETIREMENT, ETC.)

0%   1 to 5%   6 to 10%   11 to 15%   16 to 20%   21 to 30%   31 to 50%   51 to Above

DO YOU LOOK AT THE RIGHT SIDE OF A MENU (PRICES) OR THE
LEFT (FOOD DESCRIPTIONS) WHEN YOU GO TO A NICE
RESTAURANT?

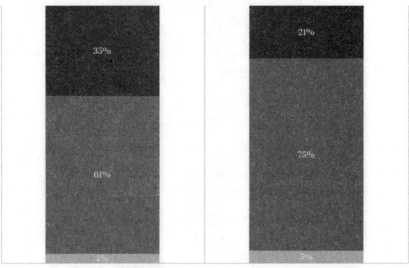

DO YOU LOOK AT THE RIGHT SIDE OF A MENU (PRICES) OR THE LEFT (FOOD DESCRIPTIONS) WHEN YOU GO TO A NICE RESTAURANT?

■ I don't go to restaurants ■ Descriptions ■ Prices

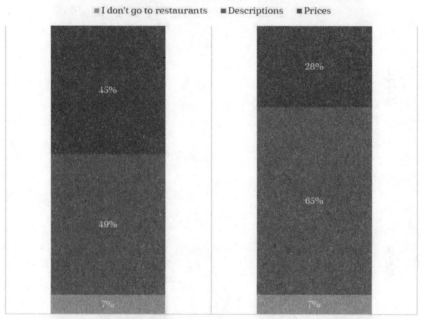

NON-MILLIONAIRES 2008   NON-MILLIONAIRE 2023

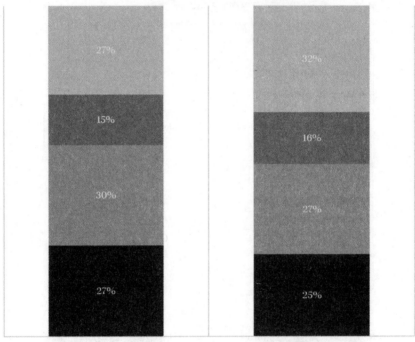

DO YOU MEDITATE OR PRAY?

DO YOU MEDITATE OR PRAY?

■ Never ■ Seldom ■ 2-3 Time per Week ■ Daily

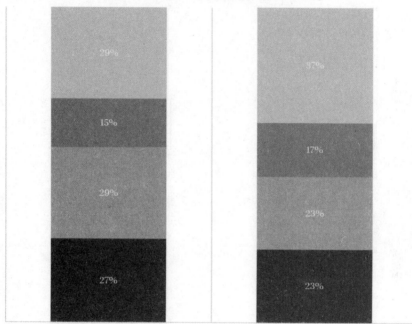

NON-MILLIONAIRE 2008   NON-MILLIONAIRE 2023

I CAN REALLY HAVE ANYTHING I DESIRE.

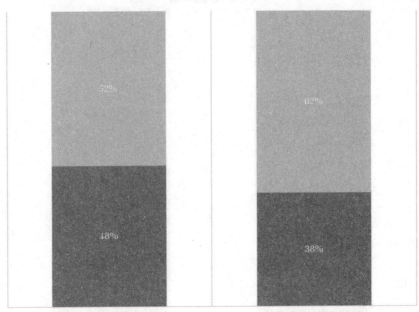

I CAN REALLY HAVE ANYTHING I DESIRE.
■ FALSE ■ TRUE

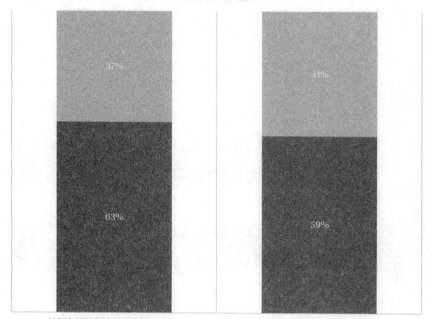

NON-MILLIONAIRES 2008   NON-MILLIONAIRE 2023

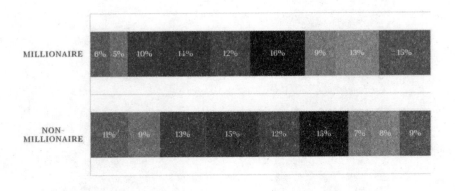

HOW MANY HOURS DO YOU EXERCISE A WEEK?

■ 0 Hour ■ 1 Hour ■ 2 Hours ■ 3 Hours ■ 4 Hours ■ 5 Hours ■ 6 Hours ■ 7 to 9 Hours ■ 10 to Above

MILLIONAIRE	6%	5%	10%	14%	12%	16%	9%	13%	15%
NON-MILLIONAIRE	11%	9%	13%	15%	12%	15%	7%	8%	9%

Disclaimer: The combined charts that do not have an '08 or '23 label include the combined participant data from the 2008 and 2023 of ~20,000 surveys as the variation between both sets of data for that question was statistically insignificant. The survey (of which the charts in this book are a small subset) consisted of approximately 100 questions, worded the same in both surveys, with approximately 5% submitting both 2008 and 2023 surveys. The data comparing those same users will be released in the next book, as well as additional questions and analysis. This data is available to license by contacting Connection@EavesdroppingOn.com

CHAPTER 6

Can a Book Change Your Life?

JACK M.
Net Worth: $1–1.25 Million
Income: $60–100k
Started Investing: 34
Attained Millionaire Status: 55

Can a book change your life? Well, if you're asking James "Jack" M., he would say yes.

He recalls growing up in the small town of Corinth, Mississippi, with a population of 13,000: "My earliest recollection, I remember a sign on the outskirts of town that said the population. I lived there for 16 years, that exact sign was still there when I left. It hadn't done much. It is primarily known for its involvement in the Civil War. Our claim to fame was Wurlitzer pianos and that *National Geographic* was printed there." Jack had the kind of upbringing that many of us baby boomers can relate to. It was typical small-town America. They rode their bicycles across town, and no one worried about where you were or what you were doing as a kid, until dinner time. The post–WWII life was a lot simpler, and a career was about finding a job with a good company and climbing the ladder. "In my hometown, if you could aspire to become the supervisor of the Wurlitzer plant, you had pretty well made it when it came to making a living in Corinth. All the family that was from there has since passed away. I was able to take my son back there one time and walk through some of the old areas that I grew up in during my childhood, and I cherish that."

When Jack was in the fourth grade, he was asked to do a book report. "I walked into the school library and came across a book that just said *Pilot* on the cover. It was about 250 pages long, and I thought I could get through that quickly, if I had to do the old book report thing. It was written by a fellow by the name of Tony LeVier. Tony was a test pilot for Lockheed. From that point on, I was fascinated with the thought of airplanes. I've got a copy of it in my hand. It has been out of print for a number of years, but I was able to do some research and find it. I bought it last year as a reminder. Growing up in Mississippi with not a lot of opportunities other than the ones you made for yourself, I had to put a lot of things on hold for a while, but it was always in the back of my mind."

The turning point in his life came after he graduated from high school and talked with his friend's brother, who happened to be a pilot. Jack picked his brain and explored all the pros and cons of pursuing a career in aviation, and after that conversation, his course was set. "Until I talked to him that night, I didn't even realize you could get paid to fly a plane."

He started going out as early as possible on Saturday mornings to the local airport, it cost him $6 an hour to rent a plane, almost a day's work for him. "I realized very quickly that that was not going to be my path to success, if I had to pay to fly myself. A mentor told me, 'If you can afford to pay for everything you need to get this job, you don't need the job. You've got to find other ways. You've got to be creative in the ways you do that.' As it turned out, Uncle Sam had gotten us into a nice little war and they needed pilots, so I volunteered." Not willing to give up on his dream, Jack decided to join the Army to get his training. He remembers driving out of town to basic training and seeing that population sign that still read 13,000, years later. He realized then that he wasn't going to live a normal life.

"I volunteered to fly helicopters for the Army, and that basically involved about a year's worth of training, then they would send you home for a little leave, then off to Vietnam. When I finished my tour in Vietnam, we were still four years away from completely pulling out, but they had already projected forward that the numbers that were needed were going to diminish. So, they offered us the option of separating from the service."

After learning to fly helicopters, he landed a job through GI Bill education benefits and trained as a flight instructor. He devoted the next few years to acquiring credentials and experience before he finally achieved his dream of working for a major airline, where he eventually specialized in flying Boeing 767s. "Staying with one thing for a long time was to some extent growing up in a kind of sheltered environment. I wasn't exposed to a lot of different possibilities, and so I saw this and said, 'Well, now, that seems like something that would just be great fun to do.' My goal when I joined the Army was to get some good-quality flight training and see what door opened up. The final goal was always to work for an airline. I look back and realize how fragile that really was, how unusual it would have been to be able to predict all the things that had to happen at that time. I feel lucky that I did make it. I lived a pretty good life."

Jack spent the next 26 years flying. Although he was a successful pilot, it wasn't until he was offered an early buyout package from his airline that he attained millionaire status. "My advisor and I had talked at great length that summer. As a matter of fact, I was in Europe for two weeks with my daughter when I had that call. We had been trying to hold onto the possibility that things would get better for the airlines or wouldn't change. But with a lump-sum option my financial advisor said, 'Look, that is probably going to go away if they go into bankruptcy.' So it turned out everything was prophetic, because it did. I took the $1 million payout and walked away. It was heart-wrenching and hard not to think selfishly, as I would have liked to keep flying, but I chose to walk away as it was a better decision for my family. I had to walk away from something I truly loved to do, and I still miss it."

Having two kids who look to him for guidance has been an eye-opener. He humbly admits, they consider him successful. "My parents never had extra money to save or invest, but I was taught that if you work hard, you will be successful." He taught his kids never to go into debt, because he never did. "I taught them to understand that there is value in saving for your future, to make sure you have enough money on hand to handle the normal and the unexpected items that come along."

This lesson was put to the test when Jack's son entered law school. At that time, they had a talk, and he asked how his son was doing financially and whether he was using his credit cards too much. His son put his hand on his dad's shoulder and said, "Oh, Pop, I pay off that credit card every month. You didn't know it, but I was listening all that time."

"A fun story about that is back when the kids were younger, I had been trying to come up with something to do as far as a college-savings plan. I was just putting money into a basic savings account for them. My local advisor called and said to look at putting some stock into the account, and it might grow quicker. He recommended a company I had never heard of that sold insurance in Japan, not in America. I bought 100 shares of stock at about $1,300. We split those shares in half and set up gift-to-minors accounts for the kids. That company was AFLAC (American Family Life Insurance). When my son graduated from law school, he sold the last bit of AFLAC to pay for law school."

He recalls having a conversation with them as they wondered about the path to success. "I told them, when I aimed at this career back at 17 years old, I didn't think it was even possible. Thirteen years later, I had accomplished it and I realized I should have aimed a little higher." He taught them that you should always aim a little higher than you really think you can go, because you can't truly appreciate the capabilities that you have until you are tested. Test yourself.

By 2008, Jack had saved about $1.4 million, but he watched the economic crisis of 2008 bring that down to $600,000. "I was using Modern Portfolio Theory. It was supposed to work, and I got awfully close to the place of taking my 5% a year and going about my business. Then when you start watching it go away, you find yourself sort of in a panic. You don't think it's going to zero, but you don't know how low it's going to go. I don't necessarily live on hope, but sometimes that's all we have left."

He thought he was diversified; but now, looking back, he sees he was only diversified across the available investment options within the mutual fund he chose, but not across different strategies.

He and his wife both continue to work, though not full-time. "The recent market activity just caused us to push retirement a little farther into the future, as it did for so many other people. I've got to keep looking at the future; I can't do anything about the past."

He had always separated his 401(k) account, primarily with the intention of establishing a self-directed IRA in order to have money available to go in other directions. "It may be time to do that." He also has about 25% of his assets in cash, the idea being that if things go south, he has enough money to live on for the next five years as he waits for the economy to turn around.

He and his wife live on about $80,000 a year and have not really dipped into their savings yet. "I can't stop myself from doing something at this time. I have an instructor job that is flexible. I am always looking for the next thing. I was just working on an airplane sales deal. I do some research and consulting work for a corporate aircraft sales business. I keep my ear to the ground. I am interested in buying into some private small business where things aren't looking good. You never know when opportunities might arise."

Jack recalls being in Vegas and watching people play at the craps table. He always thought the guy who said, "Let it ride" was an idiot. He feels the same way about how he approaches retirement. "I have changed my outlook considerably. I do not anticipate or even look forward to the day when I don't do any work; that's just not me. But I do look forward to being able to control my schedule a little better and to be able to go out and see places and do the things I haven't done."

His years as a pilot did more than just set him up financially; he also learned a valuable lesson when it comes to success: "Aim high and then adjust your aim and aim higher. Don't listen to those naysayers. You will usually achieve more than you expect."

Years later, Jack had never forgotten the significance of the book he read in the fourth grade. He keeps that copy of *Pilot* on hand to remind him of what believing in your dreams enables you to achieve.

SIX YEARS LATER ...
Net Worth Increased to $1.9 Million

JOHN: When we last talked, Jack, you were a recently retired pilot. Before the recession hit, you had a net worth of $1.25 million and were making about $60,000–100,000 a year. Then you took a hit. What has happened since then?

JACK: After retiring early at 56 from Delta because of the impend-
             ing bankruptcy, I took that position in a contracting role as a
             training pilot. I'm still doing that. I am almost 10 years into
             that position. I do it about 10 days a month on average. It's
             a nice little part-time thing.

TIFFANI: What about your investments?

JACK: I basically continued investing the way I had always been.
             I went through the down time in a fairly conservative posi-
             tion with my investments. I didn't get hurt as bad as a lot of
             people. I can imagine that after the credit crisis hit, some
             of the people on your millionaires list might not have been
             millionaires anymore.

             I entered a partnership with an old friend in the aircraft
             sales business. I specialize in helicopters, but we try to keep
             it at the turbo prop level. We seek business everywhere from
             Brazil to Africa.

JOHN: Is there anything that stands out from the time when you
             first made money from your piloting background?

JACK: Pilots, by nature, are generally very conservative people. It
             comes from having to trust a lot of airplane parts that are
             spinning and running and making noise. I came back from
             Vietnam and worked as a commercial pilot for seven years.
             That wasn't getting me anywhere financially. The main
             thing was that my conservative bent forced me to begin sav-
             ing money. I funded two college educations before my first
             child ever went to school. I stayed fully invested. It turned
             out that was the right decision.

JOHN: You stayed fully invested, what did that look like?

JACK: I have a moderate portfolio, 60/40 between stocks and
             bonds, ETFs, and cash. As I have gotten older – and John,
             we have gotten older – that mix is now 40/60.

             The equity side went down, but the loss was much less
             than the market. We stayed invested with the purpose of
             being there fully when the upturn came. We stayed positive
             through the whole thing. I always keep five years of cash
             available. My net worth is about $1.9 million now. And up
             from where it was.

TIFFANI: What would you do if you fully retired?

JACK: I would still have the aircraft sales. I can do it from anywhere and do it anytime I want to. I can talk on the telephone anywhere. I am also a director of an educational foundation. The educational part is to restore Vietnam-era aircraft and display them to the public.

It can be scary to think about fully retiring. The concept of literally walking away from everything that engages you and then not having anything to do – I don't know how people do it. I don't know how I would function if I didn't have a reason to get up every morning. An old guy flying old helicopters – I say that's probably what I'll do till the end.

TIFFANI: How do you make important decisions, like investments and the retirement question?

JACK: I try to stay informed about what's going on in the world so that I have a basis. I discuss it, research it, pray about it, and do a lot of different things that give me a sense of peace when I finally pulled the trigger and said, "Okay, I'm going to do this."

It was a difficult decision to retire from the airline. Earlier in life, I was on this train between Austria and Paris, and I had just finished reading a professor's book called *Good to Great* by Jim Collins. "You've got to know who needs to be on the bus and who needs to be off the bus." I pose that question to myself. When it will be time for me to get off the bus.

I have reached the point now where I can look back and recognize things. I had never realized when I was young that they would pay people to fly airplanes. I didn't realize that book was the beginning of it. At that point in time, *Pilot* sounded pretty romantic and it gave me a much better idea of where I was going to drive myself. Now, I try to be conscious of how important moments like that and my words can be to others. You just don't know who you are going to touch. I take that responsibility very seriously.

What is missing from your life?
Time to relax

One thing you learned about life you would want to pass down to future generations
Set priorities. Have faith in something bigger than yourself. Love your family and friends completely and unconditionally. Vary your activities to balance your life.

Stupidest thing you spent money on
Diet plans.

Favorite books
Pilot (Tony LeVier with John Guenther); *The Right Stuff* (Tom Wolfe).

SIX *MORE* YEARS LATER ...
Net Worth Increased to $2.2 Million

Jack has been one of our favorite journeys to be a part of. His spirit comes through, and the story of finding a book as a child and then living that childhood dream waxes poetic. Jack hasn't looked back since retiring. Remember when he read on a train in Europe about knowing "when to get off the bus"? He did it with Delta before the bankruptcy. He had done it again with his training job, when he realized he only spent half his time with his wife. He left that job with joy in his heart.

He does have his volunteer work with the educational foundation. That position means FAA compliance, and that is a never-ending story and does keep him busy. What about flying? He has always loved that and missed it when he wasn't involved. Well, he just purchased two self-flying airplanes and is having a lot of fun flying them.

"I am having so much fun. Everything I do, if it's not fun, I just don't do it."

Let's do some numbers. Jack's net worth has slightly increased and he is not touching his principal. The growth to $2.2 million has been acceptable, as he has some solid dividends. His downturns have tended to be smaller than the averages out there, and his upticks have followed the market.

Jack told us that he lived frugally, and he continues to do so. His income is from his dividends and Social Security. "I've never really considered Social Security as a source of income, but I am thanking my lucky stars that I have it. Those things enable us to do the things we want to do, and to not have to go out and find a job at 72.

"My wife and I work for 'Jack M. Incorporated,' we have to be very conscious of whether we are overliving or underliving our income potential, even though we've settled in, you know. After I had been retired from Delta for four years – we were still going through the pains of trying to decide that rhythm, and immediately started cutting back on unnecessary things. But if we were on video, you could tell that I haven't missed any meals.

"Overall, given the ups and downs that we've experienced over the 16 years since I left Delta, and in the four years since I left my training position with them, I've been very pleased.

"I waited until I was 68, almost 69, to start taking Social Security. That element has accounted for nearly half of our income. But at the same time, we don't have any new expenses that are leading us into that unknown territory, and we do try to avoid those.

"I'm kind of like a lot of retired people; we pay cash for things that we might have financed at one time. The house still has a mortgage on it. But that's a very manageable thing, and the interest rate is really good. I have considered paying it off, but the tax hit to take that money out of the IRA and keeping that money from working for me vs. the payments, just doesn't make sense.

"We seem to do everything that we want to do. But in retirement, what you find is that you begin to eliminate some things that you thought you wanted to do that aren't worth adding to your life. We've been satisfied, I should say, and very comfortable in the way that we live, and it fits our income stream very well. Marrying those two things up is not something you do overnight. I advise a lot of new retirees in that regard."

Now why take this risk and stay close to the market, after working so hard on expenses in his current income stream? Is it just the dividend income that is needed?

"I am fairly conservative and maintain limited exposure to the open overall market. We do keep that up to keep some growth going, and that has been beneficial. As time has passed, we have retreated and reduced exposure in proportion to age. Are we in the right place? I ask that question, and the answer is we are watching over it, and if we need to make changes we will. I am pretty satisfied.

"I have worked with a financial advisor for the last 20 years. Same person. He has kept my losses to a minimum while compensating us on the other end. As much as you can trust anybody, I guess I trust him. That is one person you have to feel good about.

"I concentrated my life on flying airplanes and helicopters. I always felt I did that very well. I wanted to be sure that the person who handled my money was equally as competent. I never tried to fool myself into thinking I could be the world's greatest investor."

Jack's kids have both had conversations with his financial advisor, something he wished he would have done at their age. They're doing better than he would have dreamed possible in so many ways. His son is a corporate attorney, and his daughter is a PhD child psychologist providing services to school children at risk. "They continue to impress me, and God bless them. I couldn't be happier for that; I could leave this world tomorrow and never worry about them at all. I am proud of them."

Jack runs into young people that will actively ask for advice. He has had the opportunity to do interviews about his flying career and his time in Vietnam. Every once in a while he will get a call from someone who watched the *History Channel* and thought there was a guy that looked like him. "Well, I just reply, 'That's because it was me.'" That ends up starting a conversation, and he realizes he never knows who he will influence.

We know Jack's story well by now: the pivotal turning point from a book in his school library, with a mentor encouraging him to just do it. In hindsight, is there anything he would have done differently?

"I had made the decision that was what I wanted in high school. Aviation brought me a certain level of joy and, almost every day, a sense of accomplishment. It fulfilled a lot of needs every human has. I was lucky in that it made me enough money to put me in a position that if something bad happened that wasn't the end of it. It set me on a course to live the life I am living now.

"I guess being that poor kid from Mississippi, I don't think I had high expectations. It took 13 years to become that pilot. Now, when you are 17 years old, that sounds like a long time. When you are 72 years old, you look back and go, 'You know, I should have set the bar just a little higher than that.'"

 ## QUESTIONS FROM OUR OTHER MILLIONAIRES

Do you think you are rich?
In a lot of ways, yes, but not money-wise. I am comfortable when it comes to money, but the richness of life comes from so many other things. Seven weeks' worth of it is currently in this house. (Jack was visiting his newborn grandson.)

What is important to you and how has that changed over time?
Roger, the mentor who first posed the question to me, over ham sandwiches one night, of what I wanted to do with my life. I was 17 years old; I had no clue. But then he asked, have you ever thought about flying airplanes for a living? He had been flying for an airline and he took the next few hours to help lay out the next 13 years of my life. He didn't tell me to do it, he just showed me a path.

As it turns out, that was very influential, and I was grateful that he had taken that much time to spend with a young man he had just met. It was a long time before I contacted him again to express how much I appreciated his making an effort. Until he passed away, we stayed in touch on a fairly regular basis. Once again, I thanked him for the wise counsel that he was able to provide me, and it has made me very aware of being able to provide that myself to others, when the opportunity arises. It would be the highlight of my life if one of these young people that I have counseled gave me a call one day and said, "Hey, you know what? I just realized you did something good for me."

Millionaires' Business Lessons

🔑 "I grew up with a father who traded the market. I was fascinated. I was about 20 years old when Mother got sick and passed away from cancer. After a brief time trying to work for my father – he was tough to work for – I left. I went to work with someone who traded gold futures and gold. I traded gold futures. I traded all that I had, and I lost. All the money that I had gotten from my mom passing, about $300,000. I had thought about trading, 'This is real easy.' I thought I was bigger than the market at that time even though I was a little punk. My friend tells me that he remembers me on the train the day I lost it, my face completely white and I couldn't believe what happened. I realized my first lesson; don't put your eggs in one basket. It probably took me about 3–6 months after that to realize it, and I was scared. I sat down and learned and really asked myself what I did wrong and go over it. I developed a tremendous respect for the market after that."

—Kevin

🔑 "An important lesson I learned from the man that took my company public. He arrived in a limousine, came in, we met for an hour. He went right back out and got in that limousine. The driver knew where to take him for his next appointment and he spent that time preparing for his next conference while he was moving – instead of renting a car, figuring out the address, etc. I started doing the same thing. I have a driver that drives me now. I gain that

(continued)

hour and a half each day by not being the driver. I recommend that for anybody who values their time. A good friend of mine mentioned that I should think about how I value my time. He said, 'If you make a million dollars a year, and you work 2,000 hours, that's $500 an hour. So, if you can hire somebody to do something for less than that, you should.' I have tried to remember that."

—Richard

"Never quit, never quit, never quit. That is number one. Number two is trusting in your fellow employees and involving them in growing the business, not just as employees, but as sort of partners. I mean partners in the best sense, not like stockholders, or other ownership like that. But figuring out that those other people are really what make you successful. Understanding that is crucial."

—Terry

"The importance of finding good people and then expanding the business to sort of match the abilities of the people we have. We've tried several things that just absolutely didn't work, but it's worth trying it different ways when you find the one that does work."

—Lowery

CHAPTER 7

The Worst Mistake or Best Decision?

Joining the Family Business

LINCOLN A.
Net Worth: $5–8 Million
Income: $200–500k
Started Investing: 12
Attained Millionaire Status: 22

The successful people we encountered have not been those who give up when things get tough. It is actually the #1 character trait our millionaires attributed to their success. Lincoln learned this lesson at a young age by watching his father go from working as a second-rate wall plasterer – who got called only if the other guys weren't available – to building a small empire. "No matter the difficulty or the challenge, my dad never gave up. He always stuck with it until he found a solution. When difficulties arose where others would throw in the towel, he remained determined. I took that to heart."

After graduating with his MBA, Lincoln began working as a management consultant. He then went into the stock market, where he endured one of the worst crashes in history when the market dropped by more than 20% in a single day. He thinks that going through that helped him in the long run to not react to the constantly changing economic environment. "It takes a bit of the fear factor out of current events."

In 1945, Lincoln's father and a friend who went to a university of mines and metallurgy had a professor that decided to start a clay pot business. He was asked to look at some clay on the other side of the state. Since his father was already in the brick business, he took some clay and tested it. His dad thought, "Hmm, this looks like a good idea."

"They decided to form a partnership at that time and bought an old barn that is adjacent to our current brick operation. On Thanksgiving Day 1945 they started laying the first brick in the first kiln and had to give up because it got so cold that day the motor started freezing on the trawl. I think that is where my dad's 'stick-to-itiveness' started."

Back then, there were 72 to 73 red brick farm pot manufacturers in the United States. They grew that business through determination, hard work, and investing back into the business. There is now only one other producer left in the United States, and it is an Italian firm.

We asked him, when everyone else was moving offshore, why did you decide to stay? He admits it was a little sentimental. "My Dad started it. And also, whenever you buy things overseas in this field, the lead times are one month to three or four. We have the ability to make it and ship it right away. And maybe I have too much sentimentality, but I think, by golly, we gotta make stuff in the United States. I will say our biggest concern right now is that energy is such a huge expense. We use natural gas to fire our kiln and that just raises your cost an awful lot. With our brick business, some years ago we developed a system to burn sawdust, which is very inexpensive fuel compared to natural gas. We can't do that with pottery, though, as it leaves a flashing on the bricks."

While Lincoln has reserves of ambition and goals for growing the business, governmental regulation of small business and energy pushed him to spend a fair amount of time and money creating solutions for those issues.

"I hired a lean engineer. We reduced our natural gas consumption about one-third the last few months with some new processes. It was about having the right burners in the system, and we discovered that once you get above 1,000 degrees, all the organics are burned out of the clay and the kiln, so it is no different … the exhaust you get at that temperature is no different than what you would get out of a burner. We are just taking the exhaust and feeding it into our dryers and then we don't have to use burners in our dryers."

We found it fascinating how his concern about future energy prices compelled him to make changes now. They also changed the kiln they used. The one they used to use had a false crown in it so that when there was hot air in the kiln from the air rising up, they would take that air out and redirect it into their dryers and save money that way. The new kiln systems didn't have that. He had an idea, talked with others, and found some folks that knew how to accomplish that as well.

Now remember Lincoln had some success as a stockbroker. How did he move to the family business? It was simply that it was his childhood dream to one day be CEO of the multimillion-dollar brick and pottery business that his father had founded in 1945. He mentioned his father had warned him about family business, and family issues, and he learned firsthand what that meant. "Until I bought control, my father's brother and brother-in-law were still here at the ages of 86 and 82 and just in the way of progress at times. The ability to grow a multigenerational family business always fascinated me. My father often dissuaded me from joining the business, because, he said, a closely held family business has unique challenges and, in some ways, more risk than other types of businesses. Part of that risk lies in not being able to implement change quickly in order to react to sudden shifts in the market, because there are too many people involved in decision-making. The fact that most of the people involved are family with very real and personal ties to the business only complicates things further. There can be a sense that people feel they have things by birthright. Now, I am the only one from my generation that is involved in the day-to-day operations."

Lincoln started as a sales manager and continued working for his father for 15 years. He did indeed end up becoming CEO after his father passed away suddenly, less than a year after a tornado had demolished part of their business. That wasn't the way Lincoln had wanted to inherit the company, and he spent the next six months in shock.

"I was crushed. You will experience this working with your father, Tiffani, but you become best friends with your dad when you work with them, maybe you are already seeing this. But then go through that and they are totally … It was very difficult. I moved into dad's office and had to clean out his desk. There were so many sentimental things that made the transition all the more difficult. I still have a lot of his awards and his diploma up in my office. Even so, I knew it was my turn. Even though I had not been dealt a good hand, I knew it was my responsibility. Sometimes you just step up to the plate, and you have to hit the balls that are thrown. You have to learn to adapt to different situations.

"Not too long after dad died, I became president of the Rotary Club, which is a pretty big responsibility and that was kind of hard, because Dad knew I was going to be president and he didn't get to see it. I wanted to do the best job for the business my dad had started, and that motivated me." Lincoln never realized how lonely and isolating being a CEO could be, when the weight of a company's future rests on your shoulders.

Because of the "unique challenges" his dad had warned him about, for many years he thought his decision to join the family business was his worst mistake. However, now that he has control of the company, he realizes it may have been his best decision.

At the time of this interview, Lincoln had set a goal to increase his business 50% over the next five to seven years. The business currently makes about $25 million a year.

With such an ambitious goal he has implemented avenues to get there. "In the past we had relied on outside salespeople in terms of independent reps that were not our employees, but we paid a commission. We didn't have control over them, in making sure customers were called on, or in finding their results. We have now completely changed our sales force; we have different types of products, anything gardening related that could be pottery. We have taken our boardroom and turned it into an account management center. We now have six people in house on the phone getting paid base plus commission, working every day on outbound sales. So, I believe that growth is the potential in one year.

"After that, it is going to get harder. I am spending time finding innovative products. We have refaced our catalog, redid our website, reinvented ourselves to set a vision of being the 'gotta have.' I use this example: we want our company to be kind of like Apple Computer, in that we have the product that is really hot. You don't go to Apple necessarily because you are looking for a better price, but you go because you want an iPhone or a Mac. I know that is a bit of a stretch, but if you can position yourself where there is no one that compares, you have a lot of advantages."

Because of this intense aim for growth, he spends his time more on his business interests than he does on personal investing. He has about $1.5 million in stocks and mutual funds, but outside of growing the business he does not have any specific investment plans. He believes that he can double his net worth in 10 years and double it again in 20 years. "I think we will be able to grow the business substantially in that time period. I mean doubling in 10 years is really 7.2% per year, if you do the compounding math. It strikes me as a reasonable return to achieve and we just work at it really hard, and I think I am good enough to do that. I may be wrong," he said with a laugh. He admits that he isn't as involved in his investing as he probably should be. Still, having the stockbroker experience from years ago, he does have a passing knowledge of what is in his portfolio and how it is invested.

Lincoln met his wife on a blind date, and after years of infertility they had a surprise pregnancy. He considers their daughter his little miracle and knows she is destined for greatness. "We had six miscarriages before she was born. They did an ultrasound on the pregnancy and said that there was no fetal pulse, you don't have a baby, we are so sorry. A week later, my wife called up the doctor and said, 'I am either pregnant' or I am having terrible false pregnancy symptoms.' And, by golly, she was pregnant. We feel very blessed because at that time it was the only time in medical history where a baby was born with no fetal pulse at gestation. So, we think we have a special kid. If she would like to do this, I think she would be great at it, but I don't know. I think she has a different talent set. I think she is destined for much greater things."

Lincoln let us know that only about 10% of disagreements with his wife are about money. "I have learned to never presume what she is thinking. She puts the style and grace in our life. I would probably live very simply if it wasn't for my wife. My wife brings a lot of fun to life. I have learned spending time together and listening each other is key. I think sometimes we get so involved in what we are doing we don't make time for each other together. I think if you work hard and make money, the money isn't the issue; it is the time together and having that same focus."

Lincoln shared with excitement his focus on giving back in his local community of about 50–60,000 people. It is the kind of community that when you go to the grocery store, you know people. Where you seem to run into people wherever you go.

"If you get involved in big national efforts, I don't feel I really make a difference. I mean you do, but let me give you an example. We just completed a building for the family and children's service here that they are naming after my father. It helps with women who are pregnant, it helps with adoption. One thing I found out is that they are helping with troops coming back. Because of these extended stays in combat areas, they [soldiers] are having psychological problems and so they are getting help. We also send our daughter to a Lutheran parochial school and that is kind of a mission for our church. If you belong to our church, we do not charge you a tuition, which is extremely expensive. We put together, recently, $85,000 for a grand piano with an accomplished music director who is great with the kids."

So, we have Lincoln working long hours, volunteering extensively, being president of the Rotary Club, and pouring into his daughter. We finally asked him what is worth the money? The answer was time away with his wife to enjoy life every now and then.

"We usually take two weeks away. The thing was, after the tornado, I think I worked for about a year without a day off. I think I worked even Saturdays and Sundays, and I got to the point where I thought, 'Well this is stupid.' So we started taking time off. We are going to Singapore next. We love Hawaii, and we were just down in Colorado this summer at the Ritz Carlton in Bachelors Gulf. Even if we can't get away, we will just go to St. Louis and stay at the Ritz for a few days." He made sure we knew that these trips include his daughter. In fact, it is very infrequent that they take a trip without her.

Lincoln has a unique situation he asked us to keep "off the record." It's something that could bring in a substantial amount of money. We asked him if that changes his lifestyle. Does he still go into work 70 hours a week? What does that mean if by his definition he has just become "rich"? If you have sensed by the rest of his life described so far, his answer won't surprise you at all: "I don't know if that changes me a whole lot. I think if you don't work, it is not healthy. I think you might have a propensity to do some things and get into problems if you didn't have a purpose in life. What might change is that my wife has been wanting to build another home, so as not to have to walk up and down the stairs."

He thinks that his conservative upbringing has positively affected his life and wants, in many ways, to see this upbringing reflected in his daughter's. "The influence our parents had on us is certainly part of her upbringing."

Lincoln has an intense workweek as CEO and says he wishes he had the ability to turn off the challenges of the business when he leaves the office. "The ability to get away from it all and relax does not come easily to me. I feel a responsibility that never ends."

In the end, he firmly believes that your abilities and drive greatly determine the success you will have in life.

SIX YEARS LATER ...
Net Worth Increased to $9 Million

JOHN: Lincoln, you are 54 now. Let's take it back to 2007. The financial crisis came along; you were worth about $5 to $8 million back then and making good money – $200,000 to $500,000 a year. What happened? Yours is a very cyclical business, I would think.

TIFFANI: I would also like to add that back then you had planned to grow your business by 50%. I am so curious to find out more. So please add that into what happened as well.

LINCOLN: The brick business is actually up, and the pottery business is more or less flat.

JOHN: Wow, the brick business is up? I would have thought it was tightly connected to home building, so it would be down. I am fascinated by your business doing well. One of the side bets I would have taken is that the brick business would have had some real issues during the crisis.

LINCOLN: We do a lot of brick, but we are also master distributors for spas and pools and fireplaces. That business has been good. We saw a downturn, but we worked to build it back up. It is a conglomerate of different things we sell. The business has done well because we focused on other areas when this or that part was down. We had a meeting last night and realized that this should be our best year out of the last five years.

TIFFANI: You said your net worth was mainly in the business, and you had a little bit in stocks. Is it still distributed the same way?

LINCOLN: I have probably grown the assets outside of the business more, but that is still accurate. My net worth is a bit up after the crisis.

JOHN: Well, that is good. What else has changed? You had some of your money in mutual funds and equities. Did you ride it out, or did you get out? How did you deal with that?

LINCOLN: I rode it out. It didn't do me any good to sell when it went down, so we just hung on and kept investing more. Yes, those investments are ahead of where they were then. A lot of people get scared, but you have to realize, it's a long-term deal. You can't let the gyrations of the market lead you to make poor decisions. I don't know too many people who can call the market. You might call it one way and then miss it the next way. You just need to be dedicated to what you're doing.

TIFFANI: You were working an intense workweek back then. Do you still put most of your time into the business?

LINCOLN: Yes, but I do more charitable things now, too. I am still on the operating board of the Lutheran Family & Children's Services of Missouri. I am on the board of a retirement community. I am president of a foundation board. I am still involved in Rotary. We are going back this evening for a big fundraiser. I am also the vice-chairman of my church. I think you need to give back.

TIFFANI: I have to ask, how is your daughter doing? She is obviously older—I think she was 10 when we last talked.

LINCOLN: She is 17, a top student, a wonderful music performer, and vice-president of her class. We are really blessed. We have a wonderful child who is extremely faith-based. She is tremendous.

I think she is at an age where she is kind of embarrassed about money. I think kids go through that. We discuss hard work and things you do. She is knowledgeable about it, but that is not her focus. She does love the things that money does. She is an avid hunter/jumper, and that is an expensive hobby. She is also a violinist, and that is an expensive hobby. She benefits from money, but she is not focused on it at all. We are extremely proud of her.

What personal character trait do you attribute to your success?
My determination and my ability to be a good communicator of my business vision

Most important lesson for financial success
When faced with the biggest challenges, I know I can find solutions. It may not be easy, but big things are often anything but easy. When you share your vision with employees and make them part of the team, you build their best efforts and best ideas into the process. One person has limited impact. A never-quit attitude is always part of a success story.

Most important life lesson
It is very important that you help others with your time, your talents, and financial contributions. Some of the real joys in life are helping make a difference in the lives of others. If we instill this in our children and lead by example there is a real joy and fulfillment. That commitment is very rewarding, makes you a better person and your community a better place to live. A difference you can make that transcends generations.

Favorite books
Sometimes a Great Notion (Ken Kesey); *Zen and the Art of Motorcycle Maintenance* (Robert Pirsig); *Jitterbug Perfume* (Tom Robbins); *Pastwatch: The Redemption of Christopher Columbus* (Orson Scott Card); *Alexander Hamilton* (Ron Chernow); *The Road* (Cormac McCarthy); *America's Bubble Economy* (David Wiedemer et al.) – this was the first book on the subject I ever read and has proven to be quite accurate over the two or so years since I read it.

SIX *MORE* YEARS LATER ...
Net Worth Increased to $15 Million Plus

"Our core principle was to be the best. Our second core principle was to be the first. To have all the new items and stock up early. When the pandemic hit, I didn't cancel any containers, and I kept ordering. I was determined this was going to work." That is how Lincoln caught us up on his business in our most recent connection. It is completely in line with his description of his father he shared with us 13 years ago; he said he took it to heart. "When difficulties arose where others would throw in the towel, he remained determined."

It seemed most of the news reports and word around our local communities highlighted a lot of struggling businesses in the new universe created by the pandemic. During these last interviews, our entrepreneurs had been figuring out how to survive. Lincoln tells us how he accomplished that since our last conversation.

Wait, we stand corrected. Lincoln emphasized, "We figured out how to *thrive*, which is even better. A big part of that was preparing the company for bad times. Then when good things happen, you are ready to roll.

"We have developed an outstanding management team over the last few years that has allowed us to scale 2–3 times our volume without difficulty.

"It led to a huge increase in sales we had developed to be able to handle. People were staying at home, buying more product for their houseplants and homes. We did spectacularly well. This time of year, we normally have holidays, trade shows, business travel. All those are canceled. I save all the expenses, and our sales volume goes way up. Great combination."

What exactly did it take to develop the management team and the ability to scale orders 2–3 times without difficulty when needed?

"We spent the time to design our service to be superior to anyone else's. We spent a ton of money on software over the past two years, and that is paying in dividends now. We developed the best visual formats for selling. We use iPad tools that let you write large orders very quickly. They are all visually oriented, and we have a website for customers who want to do it themselves. We have an inside sales team and an outside sales team. However, I am likely to pay more for sales, but I can charge more.

"Part of it was changing managers because we weren't getting the best people. It probably took five years to make it shine. And independent reps are maybe a dying breed. There are fewer and fewer people who do that. It used to be pretty common. We wanted to affiliate with the best in the business.

"I invested in those independent reps. I think I have 23 of them, or something, and they have other lines. They say that I do more for them than any other of the lines they represent. We do provide them with the best resources. I think if you treat people well and value them, I think that benefits everyone.

"But that's an investment; that takes time. You don't see an immediate return. It took a couple of years. You have to have the courage and the determination to stick through that and let those pivot seeds you planted blossom.

"Now listen, sometimes the things you work on don't work out the way you planned. So, you have to be able to pivot to the right solution. Sometimes it's not going in the direction you expected. But you take what you learned and learn from that too. And then you use what you learn to formulate a better strategy or a better vision for where you want the business to go.

"Here's a tangible example. Remember we were destroyed by a tornado, everything was gone. My father died the next year. He had most of the engineering knowledge I didn't possess, and he was a minority shareholder with uncles that were running the business down.

"We tried to reduce and shrink manufacturing. That didn't work out as planned.

"We didn't keep trying to make that work. It was, 'Okay, let's change the business.' Let's make it a total district warehouse and distribution model instead of a manufacturing and distribution model.

"I completely pivoted 180 degrees to a business where I say, 'Now, if my father walked in the door, he wouldn't know where he was.' And it was his business; he had created it.

"It is that different, but you have to find solutions to the problems or challenges you face because businesses changed. So you create a new business along the way, pivoting your business in a completely different direction than you wanted it to go. We pivoted more:

"I wanted it to be scalable, which I have achieved.

"I wanted it to have focused managers in each key area who oversee running their business unit.

"I wanted them compensated in part based on how they run their business unit.

"I wanted them to have an ownership mentality in the business.

"I wanted an inside and outside sales team.

"I invest in my people in a lot of ways, whereas maybe other businesses don't."

And to the numbers.

Lincoln is taking a substantial amount more out of the business. With those funds, he is investing in different areas and having some fun too. He also is buying out almost all of the other legacy shareholders regularly. He still has a good chunk of his net worth with an investment manager and manages some himself.

Income-wise, he lives on his salary and reinvests all his dividend income.

His net worth has definitely increased. He last reported just under $10 million. While the exact number remains a mystery, we did ask if he was worth $15 million. His response, "Easily."

There is no thought of selling his business on the horizon. If he did, it would include certain criteria. He would sell the business based on profitability. He would pull cash out, as he is overcapitalized, and then the land is very valuable in itself. It would be a three-part sale.

Just where is his horse-jumping, music-loving, singing daughter now? She ended up going to Belmont on a vocal scholarship. Then after her first semester, she decided she didn't *want* to do voice anymore. What did she do? Social justice and entrepreneurship. It was a type of double major. She is very non-money-oriented, according to Lincoln. Incredibly, she works with many people on death row and teaches entrepreneurship to women in prison. They have the tools when they come out of prison to control their destiny and have employment because they will have their own businesses.

Lincoln has gone forward in updating his estate papers. They have put generation-skipping trusts and personal trusts in play. What does that look like for his daughter?

"I don't think people have a full understanding of themselves until they are about 35. I think that is a good number. I have a clause in there to keep her from spending all her money or giving away our money until then.

"For myself, I plan to probably be working in 10 years because I like what I'm doing. I like seeing everything going on and there are benefits to having different things you can do as part of that business. And it's fun.

"I'm one of these people who has an 'I can't lose' attitude. And so, we just keep working until we find a way to make it successful. And if you're not having some failures, you're not trying enough new things. I believe that stuff carries over; I'm not sure if that makes sense, but maintaining a positive attitude is critical."

QUESTIONS FROM OUR OTHER MILLIONAIRES

Do you think you are rich?
With all the people that have gained immense wealth and those in some of these high-tech industries – no, I don't think I am rich.

How do you make important decisions?
I usually look for the best outcome for everyone involved. If we do this, what are the good things? What are the risks involved? Think it through from different avenues. If I don't do this, what happens? Am I worse off if I don't make the decision at all, or am I better off? Is it something I want to do?

(continued)

What is important to you and how has that changed over time?
How I take pride in having a business where we can employ people, provide a better outcome for them, and to be able to grow that business. I think there's a whole lot to be said for signing the front side of a paycheck. And I think we can grow the business to benefit our customers, to benefit our employees, to benefit our independent sales reps, and to benefit shareholders. I don't want to be all in it, just for me. I want there to be something in it for the people involved. I think it is a better decision that way.

Were there any significant turning points in your life, in hindsight?
Shutting down the manufacturing business was a big turning point. Buying out my cousins was a big turning point. Manufacturing, because, that was what the company was founded on, that was the core business, that was my 70% of sales, all of that has gone now.

It was risky. It's risky because you're gonna become just a distributor and not a manufacturer. You can only control a certain part of your destiny. So, you have to determine how you can better operate your business to maximize growth and profitability. Part of that's been, well, we got rid of all our big chain business. It's not profitable, you sell a lot. But it's designed to get your last dollar and it was like, forget it. So, we said good-bye to some very large customers and said, by golly, we can make this up with more customers, where we can enjoy doing business with them and be more profitable.

Quotes to Ruminate On

THE ONE THING THAT COULD HAVE KEPT YOU FROM ACHIEVING YOUR GOALS/SUCCESS?

"Playing it safe and staying in industry – settling for less than what I know I could really do and accomplish." —Ted

"If I somehow had lost my passion for what I was doing. Whether that would have happened because of personal demons (alcohol, drugs) or abject failure to achieve (disappointment, despair)." —Richard

"Not stepping outside of corporate America." —Colby

"Family tradition. Keeping money invested as it is, never taking the opportunity to sell." —Christopher

"Choosing the wrong career." —James

"Since I was consistently getting in trouble as a youth, always rebelling against authority that I did not personally feel deserved my respect, I could have either gotten myself killed, seriously hurt, or ended up in jail." —Dom

"Impulsiveness and impatience." —Virginia

"The country I grew up in (India) had a relatively closed economy in the mid-1980s, if India had not opened forex in '85 or so, to enable students to study abroad, I would not have been able to study in the US, which could have kept me from achieving my success." —Radha

CHAPTER 8

Going Debt-Free and Focusing on Doing What I Like

ALLEN A.
Net Worth: $3 Million
Income: $360k
Started Investing: 28
Attained Millionaire Status: 50

Allen's story began in a small town of 350 people in Canada, born just after World War II. His father was in the Canadian Army Pay Corps., but he had flat feet and couldn't be in the troops that would ship overseas.

His father was a bit involved in bookkeeping and ended up becoming a municipal agent for the local government. Down the line, he started a credit union on the side. He began struggling with his health, and per his doctor's suggestion that the fresh air would do him good, he was advised to work outside.

"My grandfather and two of my uncles had mink farms just outside of Victoria. So, we moved to Victoria and started a mink farm with a few minks they had given us. My father didn't like being tied up every day – twice a day to feed and water the mink, so he went back to a credit union about 60 miles north. I would say we were probably lower-middle-class. Growing up, I did a lot of skating, and played some hockey. We weren't poor, but we were far from being wealthy. My father built the house that we lived in, thanks to a very low-interest VA loan."

Because his parents grew up during the Depression, the concepts of saving and spending conservatively came naturally to him. "When I was in high school, I was saving money. They gave me money for university; I saved that. I ended up purchasing a used vehicle with some of that money once I was out and became a dentist." He reminisces about buying a BMW, but he didn't consider that extravagant, and he still does not think he is. After his divorce, there were several years he lived in an apartment in the same community as his children to help support them. During this time before he married again, he had a small 26-foot boat split with a partner and used it every week to spend time in the San Juan Islands and the Gulf Islands.

Back when Allen left the small-town life, he enrolled at university in British Columbia. "Initially I wanted to be an engineer, and so I got a degree in engineering. Then I decided that I didn't like the idea of working for a big company, so I ended up going into dentistry." It is to this kind of open-mindedness that he attributes his continued success in life. "I would start out doing everything and then slowly eliminate the things I didn't enjoy. I think I prospered more because of that, focusing on what I liked."

Twenty years ago, Allen went to a seminar by White Hill Management that convinced him to accelerate their debt reduction. They were already doing so, to an extent, and so with the extra motivation they became debt-free very quickly.

"One of the things we did was double up on our mortgage payments and make a substantial payment towards principal once a year." Having generated more available capital, Allen then became more interested in investing and began to do more reading and studying in that direction. For the last 30 years he has primarily managed their money himself.

"I would be focused for a few months and then I would sort of forget about it for a while and maybe it wasn't a good time to do that. I read your letter every week, and a few other financial letters. I wonder if I am getting too much input from too many sources. But I have done all right this way. I would have done better if I used stop losses more often."

Allen's net worth is about $3 million, and his portfolio is very diverse. He has recently decided to have someone else manage a sizable portion of his wealth. "That's because I am sometimes not as focused as

I could be. I'm going to let them manage it and see how they do. That is going to help me become better focused with the part I am going to manage. Then, I will compare and decide if I'm going to go back and manage it all myself again."

Although his income is around $350,000 a year, they live relatively modestly. Allen's income is about $10,000 a month. His wife's is closer to $20,000. Between the two of them, they spend only around $7,000 of that a month for their personal expenses, so they have a considerable amount of money left to save. "There just aren't things we feel we need to spend money on, so we figure we will save it.

"We fully intend to leave a substantial amount of money to the private school my daughter attended and to charities, and we will increase that over time." The importance of leaving a large amount to the school, is he really feels like he can get behind the vision and mission of the school. He joined the board of governors to support the mission. "We took a trip recently and we said 'OK if something happens to us on this trip, we want a million dollars to go to this school.' But that was not an irrevocable setup. We realized we need to reorganize and set some things up. I envision our estates to increase even after we retire, rather than decrease."

His assets are currently divided between 75% cash or cash equivalents and the money that is invested, which is primarily in stocks, with a lot in fairly small-cap. He would also like to increase his position in gold. "I think it was a few months ago, I was listening to *Money Talks*, and reading your weekly letter, and I decided going to cash would probably be the best route to take. I am pretty confident going forward. Part of the reason, at this point, is that I am being fairly cautious. I think there will always be opportunities and I sort of come from an abundance, rather than scarcity viewpoint. Not that I am going to do things foolishly, but as long as we can get through the next little while, there will be opportunities to make more money. In the meantime, I will be more cautious."

Allen sold his practice in the small community where they live but stayed on for a while at two days a week. "My lawyer had said that it is quite likely that the buyer will be happy enough and he will want you out of there. Well, the worst is happening, he wants me to stay on. So, I have the two days a week. On selling, I felt that I might be better off if I was out of the practice, part of it was I want to be closer with my daughters. In addition, I felt that we were in a good enough position, financially, to do it. I wanted to spend more time managing our money. We have this other home on the island near us, and I have done a lot of the building and there is more I want to do.

"Now, my wife spends a lot of hours at her office. We are trying to decrease the number of hours she spends. I think she will continue for a while. She feels a very strong obligation to her patients and there is a real shortage of family physicians where we are. In addition to that, our 20-year-old daughter may go into medicine. If she does, then my wife will probably continue practicing until she gets out. So that is another six or seven years before retirement. But she is taking a little more time off. The past year she took about 16 weeks off. Part of that was holidays, but she is also involved with soccer. She is the team doctor for the women's professional soccer team here. As a result of that association, she has gone to Mexico and Chile for a number of tournaments. So that is part of the time off, which I encourage her to do.

I also have this satellite dental practice on the island. There are only about 1,000 people and they don't have a dentist. I started a part-time practice about 20 hours a month there. I will phase out of the practice I sold, but I will continue to practice on the island for several years."

Allen gave his children a book called *The Wealthy Barber* when they were younger and believes they took its concepts to heart. He believes his daughter will be successful financially and it won't be an issue. His son, he believes, has Asperger syndrome. "He is high functioning. I have offered that if he wants to go back to school and do more than he is doing now, I would like to help him with that."

Even though he has always encouraged them to be conservative in their spending and to not accumulate debt, he admits that the youngest daughter may be a bit more extravagant because of where they stand financially. "I am not sure of all the reasons, some of the things she spends money on, we are not so happy about, but she knows where we are coming from. She is aware of our finances. She knows how we live, and I think that she is becoming more conscious and more responsible. We have talked to them about this and I can see it coming through."

Staying active is very important to Allen. He loves boating and has even run several marathons. "I enjoy playing tennis. I ran my first marathon in '77, I did the Boston in '78. I did about 11 marathons in 3 years. I did reasonably. 2:48 was my best time, so it wasn't too bad. The athletics has continued to be an interest of mine throughout my life, as well as my wife. I try to get in half an hour of exercise a day to stay in shape."

In the end he says that he chooses to focus on what he excels at rather than trying to be all things to all people. "I can't do everything, and I've learned that I must delegate. I could probably do more of that, but I'm still learning."

Reaching this financial status has adjusted his viewpoint a bit. "I don't think much about making purchases, but I do think about how things would improve life for me. I don't do things I don't like to do as much. I think Will Rogers said that he never met someone he didn't like, but that didn't mean he necessarily wants to spend time with them. So, I think I am becoming more selective in the time that I spend with people and who I spend that time with. I also enjoy building things. I have built houses and furniture. There are some things I have come to realize that I can't, well, I can't drive a bobcat as well as some other people do on a regular basis. So rather than me doing all that stuff myself, I will hire someone to do it. In the areas that I am proficient in building, I often get frustrated if I hire someone else and they don't do it well, and I end up having to do it myself, again. But there are some areas I am realizing, I can't be all things to all people, or do all things myself. I am finding it a little easier to delegate.

"I know that I have certainly done that in my career and industry. I started out basically doing everything there and then eliminated the things that I didn't enjoy. I think I prospered more because of that, focusing more on what I liked."

SIX YEARS LATER ...
Net Worth Increased to $7 Million

JOHN: You're 68 now. The credit crisis and the Great Recession came along; what happened to you?

ALLEN: As a result of listening to *Money Talk* and Michael Campbell and some of the stuff that you were writing in *Thoughts from* *the Frontline*, I went pretty much fully to cash in 2008, prior to everything going down. I therefore survived that very well. Subsequently, I handed over a lot of our finances to a management company you actually introduced me to. I am now somewhat less active in managing our finances myself, even though I have since retired.

One of the reasons why I stopped being as involved in my finances is that, first, I feel we have enough that I don't have to worry about it. Then, I think our wealth manager is doing a good job for us. I have time now to do some other things that I want to do. For instance, I continue to volunteer for the private school I mentioned previously, that our daughter graduated from a few years ago.

TIFFANI: I want to bring you back. In our first conversation you were going to put some of your assets with an investment manager and compare it to how you did on your own. How did that experiment go?

ALLEN: I think the thing was that we decided we were secure enough; we had enough funds, and there were other things I wanted to do rather than focusing a lot of attention on financial management. I continue to read a lot of newsletters from various sources, but there are other things I want to do. I feel that if I managed it myself, I'd need to put in more time than I want to. So, I kept investing with money managers.

JOHN: What are you doing now? What does your day look like?

ALLEN: A lot of it with my community. The volunteering at the private school – I am on the board of governors, and I probably spend 40 to 60 hours a month doing that. In addition, my wife has talked me into doing some financial management of her medical practice and a prenatal clinic she is involved in. In addition, I still enjoy building things. I have taken some training courses with a brand of woodworking tools out of Germany.

We also have a boat – a 42-footer – in partnership with another couple, so I am doing maintenance work on that and spending some time on it. We have a weekend home still on the island, and we go there often. This is our sixth boat and we have had three of each, power and sail boats. This one's sort of a trawler style. It cruises about 8 knots with a lot of comforts. It is a well finished boat. We keep it at a port in Washington. I live virtually on the US border, so it takes me about 10 minutes to drive there. I can ride my bike and even run there. When it comes to the border, I have a Nexus card and we use that to cross by boat, plane, and car.

JOHN: I am curious. If you drive your boat from US to Canadian waters, does anyone notice?

ALLEN: You can use telephone clearance. If we have people on the boat that do not have Nexus, we do have to go clear customs, but if everyone has a card we phone it in with no issue. It works the same coming back.

JOHN: Your wife is still working, so you are still saving some. At one point you'll just live off the returns from your savings. Let's talk about your net worth and investments.

ALLEN: I would say my net worth is around $7 million.

JOHN: So your assets are up substantially since the crisis.

ALLEN: Yes. We have over $4 million with the manager you introduced me to. Then there is the value of our home, the value of my wife's practice, and some of the investments that I've kept back to manage myself. The manager had a pretty good run, not bad. I think the average return was about 7%.

JOHN: Well, good for you. The crisis didn't seem to slow you down at all.

TIFFANI: So the majority of your income is coming from your gains and dividends?

ALLEN: My wife and I continue to have a fairly low-cost lifestyle. I am drawing a salary from her corporation, which at this point is about $30,000 a year. She is drawing a salary of about $60,000–$70,000. And money comes in through our investments. We tend to save about $150,000–$200,000 a year.

JOHN: How long do you think she will continue to work?

ALLEN: That is a question I have asked her several times. She knows she doesn't need to work for the money, but I expect she will work for another three to four years. She thinks she will have a more difficult time transitioning into retirement than I did. She is still working 60–70 hours a week with her general practice and obstetrics. I am 68 and she is 62.

JOHN: There is no reason to retire other than if she wants to.

ALLEN: Exactly. Right now, she wants to keep going. She even has a shoulder surgery and at some point her knee, which she will delay as long as she can. I don't think either one will stop her from practicing.

TIFFANI: I wanted to ask you about your daughter. How is she doing? How is her financial world?

ALLEN: She is not managing her finances yet. She is taking a slow way through university. She is a competitive cheerleader after a history of competitive gymnastics. She is taking a partial load and coaching three teams in competitive cheer. She competes on a university team and a community team herself. They went to the Cheer World last year in Orlando on ESPN. I went down to watch that.

When we wound down our family trust, it ended up that we owed her and my son a fairly substantial amount of money. So, we give her money every year, and some of that we are putting in a tax-free savings account that we have in Canada. Right now, that is invested in an interest-bearing account and, so, getting very little. However, I think I am going to start working that account using recommendations from a company up here. They look at small-cap companies that are earning money as opposed to the blue-sky types.

After she is finished, I may help guide her into managing stuff on her own.

JOHN: We had a nice chat about your activity level. Let's close with what you are doing for exercise these days?

ALLEN: I get at least a half an hour a day of something. I have two rowing machines – one here and one at our weekend home – I have an elliptical machine, and I run and cycle. I also feel that at this stage I need to start maintaining some muscle mass, so I have a Bowflex and a TRX system that I use.

What has changed in life as a result of achieving millionaire status?
I have made significant lifestyle purchases, such as a boat, that I wouldn't have made before. I don't believe we are extravagant, but I don't think as much about making purchases now, though I do think about how these things would improve life for me. I don't do things I don't like to do as much.

Most important life lesson
Relationships are the most important thing in life. It is an old, clichéd statement, but I don't think many people grow old wishing they had spent less time with their kids.

Greatest threat to an individual's wealth accumulation?
Instant gratification.

Favorite books
Dune series (Frank Hebert); E.E. Doc Smith science fiction; *Prince of Tides* (Pat Conroy); *Healing Heart* (Norman Cousins).

SIX *MORE* YEARS LATER ...
Net Worth Increased to $10 Million Plus

Let's recap. We left Allen, he was almost retired, spending a lot of hours on the board of governors at his daughter's school, time at his home on the island near him, and being physically active. The passage of six years has shown us that, with our millionaires, we can't predict where they are now. So, we started in the usual fashion. Allen, what is life like now? What has happened during these past years?

"Well, I left the board of governors at the school that my daughter had gone to. I am now with a local government body on the main island near me. We have a little over a 30-acre parcel there that I am playing excavator on. I have a dump truck, things like that."

Last we heard, his daughter was taking the slow route through college and was extremely involved in competitive cheerleading, and finances weren't at the top of her mind. She is still a competitive cheerleader; just now, with a bit of damage to her body from all the work she put into it, she coaches. She started saving money herself. She maxes out her Canada Tax-Free savings account, without their help. She spent a while trying to decide what she wanted to do with her life, and that blossomed into wanting to be a nurse, so she has started that process.

And now, the numbers. Allen's net worth has grown to $10 million these last six years. They still don't draw down on their principal. Their manager has continued the steady pay of 7% a year growth. They did buy a few new cars, a Ford F-150 (this must be for all the playing he is doing on the 30-acre parcel), and a Tesla Model Y.

"You know, we will never run out of money, and we'll leave a substantial amount for our children. One thing we have done is gotten my son's daughter into a private school that is similar to the one our daughter went to. We are overjoyed about that.

"Our daughter knows how much has been saved for them. Our son has an idea. When we set up our family trust, we ended up setting up shares for both of them. We give them about $30,000 a year from the money, winding down the trust. He has an idea of what sort of money he needs, and we figured we might as well give it now, rather than wait for later. The way it works in Canada, is after 21 years you have to adjust, otherwise there are some tax implications. Initially it was created when they were minors. When our daughter turned 18, it wasn't beneficial. As a result of winding it down, we ended up owing them [because of their shares], about $600,000 each."

Allen's wife was supposedly a few years away from retirement. Well, it has been six more. The building where she has her private practice, though, is for sale. If that happens, she will continue with her obstetrics and finally space out her time to one full day. Allen fully expects that to go on for another 2–3 years.

"She enjoys it. Her actual concern is one of her former partners talked about older physicians that shouldn't be practicing but haven't stopped. She is always reading up, and she is concerned that that could happen. She wants to do all she can to prevent it, so she will stay aware of that."

We have to throw in that Allen has added some weight training to his active aerobic activities. He thanks John for creating the impetus, when he read John had done 65 push ups on his 65th birthday.

There were so many turning points, in hindsight. Leaving engineering and moving to dentistry, realizing he wants to do work with people and not for someone else, separating and divorcing his first wife (as he never would have met his current wife), are watershed moments he can recall on the spot. The property on the island led to discovering enjoyment in building furniture and making things that had started in high school. Getting involved in his daughter's school led to being on the board of governors, where he felt he spent a lot of time doing things he enjoyed and contributed to the school and to the kids that graduate and go on into society. The weekend seminar that spurred the debt reduction to get his finances to where they are today. A big part of that was the decision to turn over managing his own money so he could do the things he enjoys.

There is always a moment in our interviews when the tone changes from comfortable sharing to a distinct sense of excitement to be able to share. When Allen started talking about his building projects, that excitement came through.

"This weekend, I cut a piece of maple wood into visible sections. You are just going through a tree, and it was about 3 inches thick. I ran it through my thickness sander, and then sanded it some more, and some more. I put some finishing oil on it. I have been teaching my neighbor how to make a countertop for his house. We have been putting up posts to put on his deck, instead of metal railing. I help them with my drill press. I enjoy doing all these different things. Sometimes I feel like I am helping other people more than getting anything done around here. But my wife has wanted a new kitchen for a while, and that has moved up the list."

Final thoughts, Allen, on this financial journey?

"I never could have imagined when I was in high school, or even at university, being in the position that we are in now financially. I know that a part of that is because, up until now, I haven't tended to spend very much."

QUESTIONS FROM OUR OTHER MILLIONAIRES

Do you think you are rich?
Well, I wouldn't say I am rich, because I can think of people who have maybe 10 times or even more than 10 times the amount of assets we have. On the other hand, what I have is considered rich to other people. I know my daughter thinks we are.

I do feel rich in this sense. I have these things that I can do, things I have plans to do, and without the wealth we have accumulated, we would not be able to do that.

What is important to you and how has that changed over time?
Spending time with people is more important to me than it used to be. It's not as important to me as it is to my wife. I mean, we did the Myers-Briggs thing you sent, and I could see it, and I realized why she liked to go to public gatherings, parties, and stuff like that because it energized her. Whereas it wasn't such a big deal to me. And, while I used to feel guilty about doing them or trying to avoid them, I realized that it's important for her, so it's OK for me. I am finding that choosing the people I want to spend time with, that I enjoy, is more important to me now than it used to be.

How do you make important decisions?
I certainly involve my wife, or she involves me. As far as finances are concerned, I tend to do more of the initial legwork to think about what we should do, and then we talk about it.

For other decisions, I do a lot of research. I talk to people who I think may be more expert in the area I am interested in, or even someone who is intelligent. We will bounce ideas back and forth. What one person says can inspire someone to think of something else, even just a small, little thing.

eavesdropping on
Millionaires – Their Early Years

 "I decided to be rich in the fourth grade when my father, who was in the Air Force, took my shoes to be repaired and couldn't afford the 50 cents it cost and we walked out, leaving the shoes. Almost at that moment, I decided that money was never going to be anything that I needed to worry about."

—Bob

 "I asked for a raise when I was three years old, selling popsicles."

—Desmond

 "Really not that very high expectations of what people could or should do ... [I came from] a background which thought you get a job, work there for 30 years. [This was] sort of influence of the post-war welfare state society in Britain, rather than people doing that much themselves ... But there was one person I knew from age 11 to 16, a charismatic history teacher, who just changed my expectations about what I could do. A very simple example would be it had never even occurred to me that I would go to university, and to him it was obvious that of course I would. It just changed my perspective on what I could achieve."

—Stuart

(continued)

"Never give up. Try again when you fail. Get the best deal possible on everything you buy. These ideas were learned at my father's knee. He was an expert negotiator, and I was allowed to accompany him when he was traveling around and making buying trips."

—George

"Never had a paper route but I worked for my allowance and then I started working at 14 at a paint store downtown and McDonald's, mowing the lawn, anything to make a buck. And from about 14 on I had a job if I wanted money."

—Al

"As a teenager I basically stacked lumber at the mill with the guys and made whatever minimum wage was then. I did that all through high school and through college in the summers. Mostly just manual labor. Dad wanted me to do all the manual stuff first. I didn't do any management or anything until I came back 14 years later."

—Lowery

"My folks told me they would help me go through college. I would be the first person in either family to go to college, but you got to work. I paid for about two-thirds of my college education myself. I am talking brutal, hard, physical labor because that is all there was. I had a job as a hay baler on an alfalfa ranch. Once they had it cut, dried, and rolled, they would go out with a baler with a guy on the trailer hitched to it. Wire tie bales, 100 pounds a pop. You used hay hooks, you took the bales as they came out of the bale shoot, and you stacked them on the wagon. We would typically put 2,200 to 2,400 bales a day starting at 7 a.m. to 6 p. m, with an hour for lunch. Six days a week, all summer long. Every penny I got for that job went towards college. I got paid $1 an hour (1961). I got lucky a couple of years later with a job at the forest service in Northern California and the money I made that summer paid for a whole year of school, which was great. I ended up getting my master's degree."

—Stephen

CHAPTER 9

Don't Let Complacency Keep You from Achieving Your Goals

TOM Z.
Net Worth: $3.5 Million
Income: $120K
Started Investing: 41
Attained Millionaire Status: 50

Growing up as a middle-class kid, Tom. never went without, but his family wasn't wealthy. He remembers being keenly aware of the day his parents got their paychecks in his home when most kids his age had no concept of money whatsoever. He says this is because his father never shied away from explaining things to him. It's from his father that Tom developed his principles and his work ethic. "I got all my values and life lessons from him. Education was the key to success in my dad's mind, and I went on to become the first college graduate in my family."

Tom's father worked for Chevron; Tom followed in his dad's footsteps after getting his MBA and went into the oil industry. "I was familiar with that world, since I had grown up in it." His father was a geologist who would find the oil, but Tom put his MBA to work on the financial side, taking the crude oil and making it into something. He found his niche and continued working in that industry until his retirement.

Tom began accumulating wealth by taking advantage of his company's matching program. "If I put in a buck and bought stock, they would put in a dollar and quarter. If I didn't buy the stock, they would still put in – but a dollar. At one time I think Philips had one of the highest percentage of employee-owned shares of anyone out there. That was their goal back then. So, I saved that way, I did the max – which was about 7–8% plus their match, since I was 30."

The majority of his net worth is from this savings plan, and the largest chunk of his money came from his defined-benefit plan. He took the lump sum when he retired and put it into an IRA totaling about $1.2 million. That matching savings plan had grown to an additional $900,000. His parent's inheritance kicked in and added $400,000–500,000.

He still has quite a lot of stock options that he has 10 years to exercise from the date of issue. They are in the money, with his strike price at $22 [*Strike price* is a fixed price that he can buy regardless of the current price of the stock; *in the money* represents a profit will result from the current market price vs. his strike price], and he will start looking to exercise them in year 9 or 10 of the date of being issued. "I have some I exercised in different years. My feeling is that the price of energy is only going to go up. I don't see any downside. The P/E is less than 6 currently. That is certainly low, so even if it goes up to 9, I am good. I don't need the cash. If I needed the cash that would be a different story, but I am going to hold them and try to exercise in the 9th or 10th year. The value they are currently at is about a million-five. So that is another huge chunk."

At the time of this interview, Tom said his portfolio was about 80% in stocks. "I think to sell out right now would be foolish. I'm retired. I haven't had to tap into my IRA yet and probably won't for a few years. We don't need cash, so we can look at holding on for the longer term."

When he was younger, he tried his hand at managing part of his IRA. "I did a lot of tech stuff, and of course I rode it way up and wasn't smart enough to get out, so then I rode it all the way back down.

"That's when I got out.

"That made me realize that trying to do this yourself requires skills and abilities that I don't possess. That was when so much information on computers was starting about finance, just tons of information, and a lot of it was conflicting. How long and how much do you want to read? People were making decisions instantly, and someone would push a button to buy or sell. I felt that in order to be successful at it, it was a full-time job. You literally had to be in front of the computer 24/7 watching your portfolio. I decided that wasn't for me. I didn't have the temperament, patience, knowledge, or skill.

"So, when I retired, I interviewed three companies to manage my money and then chose one. I now let them manage it all. He has all my money and makes all the decisions. Although I can call him up and tell him to do something and he will do it, but then he would back away from measuring me from his benchmark. I have never done that. I don't look but once a month at a statement I get. I can call if I have an opinion, but the money managing is not on me anymore."

"The manager is either all in equities or not at all. When he is not in at all, he will go to selling calls, to take advantage of the down market, but that is still equities to me. The other two guys were a combination of, 'What is the risk you are willing to take?' and 'How long do you want to invest?' and 'How old are you going to be?' – that kind of deal."

He placed about $2 million with the manager four years ago. It is currently up to $3.2 million. "That is not bad. If you paid attention to the DOW, S&P, and NASDAQ over that same time, that returned I think average 22–23%. Even now, with all those three indexes way down, I am still up a little bit. I have lost about a million, though, since this latest fiasco in the markets."

"My manager was quite bullish on the 3rd and 4th quarters; he gave a lot of reasons. He missed that call. He sent a letter out last week to investors about what he thought was just an absolute panic. His advice was to hang in there, and it was a mistake to sell or go to cash. I don't know, there are days that make you gulp a little bit. You can always look back at what you could have done. You just got to have faith and trust in the guy that you are paying all the money to make those decisions."

Now, he fully admits if it was another 60% drop, he would have a lifestyle change. They wouldn't take the trips or buy the new car. "All the things that spur the economy, we would have to cut back on those. It would then be, 'Am I going to outlive my money?' type thing. Right now, I don't think I will.

"Now one of the reasons I formed a little real estate business is to diversify more. My partner and I put in about $600,000. We will go to a million; that is the game plan. We paid cash for two homes in Williamsburg to rent them out. They are rented now. The plan is to buy more, but we are just waiting for the right price. We will get loans on those first two for a down payment on the third. We go in there and we give fairly lowball offers, and two people had to sell their homes that had been on the market for a long time. They eventually sold them to us. So those are income-producing rental properties, just peanuts right now."

Tom still gets a check for about $10,000 from his dad's trust every quarter, thanks to some active oil wells. He knows when oil falls back from its high, that payment will fall back as well, because it is generally based on the price of crude.

Tom and his wife have expenses of about $10,000 a month. "Outside of purchasing a car, or something like that ... we probably spend about $120,000–$130,000 a year. We try to take one or two trips a year. We just got back from Singapore. We lived there when we were overseas. The WM Alumni association has a group that kind of goes all over the world, and we take some trips like that."

Before they passed away, Tom's parents, facing a hefty estate tax, began gifting all the children and grandchildren at the maximum level, and that gave each of the kids a nice little nest egg. Tom forced his kids to save it. "I would not let them spend it when they were younger. Not on a bicycle or a car – it was savings."

Upon their high school graduation, he told his kids he would pay for their undergraduate degrees but told them paying for their graduate education was their responsibility.

Fortunately, both went to state schools. Each of them went on to get a graduate degree. "My daughter is a veterinarian. She spent four years at Texas A&M. I told her that was on her. If she really wanted to become a doctor, tuition is on her. I told her, 'I will buy a house as an investment, and you can live in the house for free during school and I will give you a monthly allowance for utilities of $200–$300 a month."

They could choose to either use the money that they had saved or borrow money through the government programs. The interest rate on that is low, so obviously you are not going to take your savings, if you can borrow at 1.5% and pay that for a long time." They both chose to use the estate money towards a home.

He attributes the fact that they saved more than he did, at that age, to how he talks with them about money. "We weren't wealthy by any means. I can remember growing up and my mom and my dad telling me, 'It's pay day.' When I was a kid towards the end, my dad did retire. He opened his own independent geologist business in Northern Oklahoma and did very, very well. So, when they started gifting their estate to us and our kids, it was not for buying anything. It was for them to put away for a rainy day."

When it comes to leaving money to his own children, Tom has a strong opinion. "When we met with our lawyer, he asked how much we wanted to leave to our children.

"I said, 'Nothing.'

"If I do, that's wonderful, but I'm not going to draft my will and make my investment decisions with the sole focus on leaving my children a nice nest egg. That is up to them. We have given them an education, and I don't feel obligated to leave them anything."

John interjected the old story: "There was a reading of a will, and the relatives came in and were wanting to know how much money they would get. The lawyer opened the envelope and read, 'Being of sound mind and good judgment, I spent it.'"

Tom said that was his philosophy as well. "My goal was when I retire, to maintain my lifestyle. People normally cut back on their lifestyle because they don't have the income coming in. I thought, no, I don't want to do that. Especially the first 10 years. I am still young.

"After watching my parents go through retirement, the last five years of their life, they didn't spend anything. They couldn't travel, they weren't buying cars; they were selling cars. What they lived on in the last 3–4 years of their lives versus the previous 10–15 years, was substantially lower. So, if you graph it, my suspicion is the same. We are spending $130,000 a year now? I am going to guess that 10–15 years from now; we will spend nowhere near that."

Tom's political viewpoint has adjusted as he accumulated more money. "When you are 25 years old and you don't have much, you don't care about policies and politics in general. You may be idealistic one way or the other. I didn't pay attention to that sort of stuff. When you start accumulating wealth, you start paying more attention to that. Tax policies, politicians promising this or that, capital gains tax, etc. They do affect decisions one might make. It is the same with my kids. If you go to them today, they don't care. Even though they are saving a lot more than I did at that age, they really aren't tuned into it that much."

Complacency, he told us, would have been the single most likely thing to have kept him from achieving his goals. We will let Tom leave you with the one thing he has learned about life that he would want to pass down to future generations: "All your successes in life are due to others. Therefore, treat everyone you meet with respect."

SIX YEARS LATER ...
Net Worth Increased to $3.6 Million

JOHN: You had a net worth of about $3.5 million. You were mak-
         ing around $120,000 a year, and then the crash hit. Tell us
         what happened.

TOM: I had all my retirement money with the one money manager.
         He invested it for me, and I was in an all-equity division.
         When the crash hit, I lost 40%; but I got it all back about
         a year ago. Now I'm ahead. If you benchmark me with the
         S&P, I'm ahead. Things kind of average out at the end of
         the day. If you stay with it long enough, we'll all be within a
         few points. I took a pretty big hit, as did everyone. It took me
         six years plus to get it all back, but I'm probably $400,000
         ahead of where I was before the crash.

JOHN: The people we've talked to have fallen into three groups.
         One big group includes those who got out, shorted, made
         money, and restructured. The other big group includes the
         ones who rode it all the way down and then rode it back
         up. The one sad group are the ones who rode it all the way
         down, then got out. Fortunately, that's the smallest group.

TOM: I've talked to the manager. He took a huge hit himself. He
         kind of prides himself for getting out when it is really bad,
         and he pleaded with us to not get out. He thought it would
         come back fast.

I mean, it scared me to see my retirement go down 40%. I could see why people got out.

I am still in 100% equity. My portfolio now is $3.6 million. I had a mental number of $4 million. I was going to get out and put it in fixed assets where my principal was preserved, and I could live off 5%. I could live off of that pretty well.

JOHN: Are you still working?

TOM: Well, I went back to work. I retired for two years, then a group approached me about 18 months ago to be CFO of a biotech start-up company. It has been in business since 1999, but the product they are selling has only been around three years. They needed some help, so they came to me. I'm not making a huge sum. I wanted cash plus equity, so that if they sell the business, I could win on that. But I am working.

JOHN: Why would you risk another potential rundown of 20 or 30% that could take you seven or eight years to get back?

TOM: That's a good question. If this company I'm working for now had a capital bid, I could win, and therefore I would ride it down. I would have enough cash to live on as I rode it back up. But you're right. Where do you draw that line? I am drawing it at $4 million. Should I draw the line at $3.6 million today, saying that the market is getting ready to go down? I don't know.

JOHN: There are places to put your money to work at $3.6 million. The difference for an annual lifestyle at 5% is just $20,000 a year. I don't think that would change your life. But what would change your life is if your net worth went down. To me it looks like your risk/reward is pretty high. You should at least have some kind of mental trigger that says, "I can take this much pain and/or I'll get back in after a correction." You should have some hedges. For all intents and purposes, you ran the race and you won. Stop running!

TOM: That is exactly what I have been thinking.

TIFFANI: All right, Tom, where are you getting your income right now?

TOM: I had put that $2 million with the manager in 2004. In the interim, I had stock options with the company I worked for that I sold and got cash from. There is still the cash from my parents. I had been living off those stock options that I've cashed in. I'm now out of stock options.

My father had a few oil wells out in Oklahoma and Texas that are still pumping, so I still get that royalty check once a quarter.

Then I started working a little bit and making some cash there.

You're gonna love this. I am down to my savings account of about $30,000, and I spend probably $12,000 a month. I am getting ready to go to my manager and say that we need to start withdrawing.

But to answer your question, I have been living off of stock options and inheritance. The real estate business here in Williamsburg, Virginia, that we bought a couple of houses and rent them out, that will just be a capital gain when we sell the houses. They aren't generating that much income right now. However, if I cashed out, I would get about $200,000.

TIFFANI: I know this has nothing to do with anything. But, what is the best pizza place there in Williamsburg? I remember reading something about pizza in Virginia?

TOM: Jamestown Pie. They also make fruit pies, but their pizza is out of sight. They make not just the traditional pizzas, but they make seafood pizzas and that kind of stuff.

TIFFANI: Thank you, I am on a 'try every pizza place in Dallas' kick. So, I'll jump back into my next question. In our previous interview you said that when you were doing your wills you didn't plan on leaving anything to your kids. Is that still your mentality?

TOM: We really shouldn't have to. They are both professionals. When I was their age, I didn't need anything. I will probably leave them something. My wife will be left behind, so I will leave them something to help support her. But to answer your question, I do not feel compelled to have an investment strategy that leaves my kids a million dollars each.

TIFFANI: So you are going to start drawing on your investments. If you are not going to leave them anything, what are you going to do with your money?

TOM: Well, if I die tomorrow, they'll get it. If we both pass away in the next five years, there will be a lot left for them. I'm saying that's fine. What I don't want to have is a strategy that says I'm only going to withdraw so much, and I'm not going to touch $2 million because I want to give each of my kids a million. Then, instead of $3.6 million, I only have $1.6 million to play with. I am just saying that whatever is left, they each get half. I don't feel compelled to have an estate planning strategy to leave to my children.

TIFFANI: But you do have a will and a trust set up?

TOM: A will yes, but not a trust.

JOHN: What is your lifestyle these days? How much do you live on now? Let's see, it was about $12,000 six years ago?

TOM: We probably spend $12,000 to $15,000 a month. We still travel a lot. I went to Florida a couple of weeks ago and rented a big house for the whole family.

            We don't live an extravagant lifestyle. I did buy a new car this year, but I'll probably drive it for the next five or six years. We eat out a lot.

            Our lifestyle went up when I retired, because we don't cook as much anymore, and we travel more. I probably spend more today on a monthly basis than I did when I worked. So, we have seen zero drop in lifestyle.

TIFFANI: How are your kids doing financially? Do you talk to them about finances?

TOM: My daughter is still a veterinarian. She is single and just moved to Charlottesville. She has a house that she just sold in Arlington, Virginia. She is not married, but she has a very nice 401(k) and a ROTH IRA, so she has been saving for years.

JOHN: Her house in Arlington probably made her a little bit of money.

TOM: Yes, about $100,000. She bought it in '04. Rode it up and then rode it down. There are a lot of young professionals in the DC market going in and out doing consulting and working with the government. They didn't really get hit too hard in the property crash. She did well.

My son has an MBA. He followed my path and works for TIAA-CREF in Charlotte, North Carolina. He just got a big promotion and a raise. He is doing the 401(k) stuff as well. I don't really get into his finances too much. I do my daughter's, so I know more about hers. But my son and his wife just built a house in Charlotte, so they are doing fine.

TIFFANI: All right, for fun, what is the stupidest thing you have ever spent money on?

TOM: Easy answer. Years ago, I brewed my own beer and went out and bought a big NEW refrigerator to keep my bottles of beer cold. Paid way too much (could have bought a used one for practically nothing). Three years later the compressor went, and the repair guy said it would cost more to fix it than to buy a new one. Wasted $1,200.

Your best mistake
I tried to manage my own IRA during the dot-com era. Made a lot of money then lost it all before I could get out. I realized that buying stocks was easy but knowing when to sell was hard. I became married to my choices and refused to admit defeat. So, the mistake was trying to do it by myself without proper discipline or knowledge (too much information on the internet). So that wound up working to my advantage, as I turned over all those decisions to a money manager to manage my portfolio for me.

Most important life lesson
Be a saver, not a spender. We live within our means. The only debt I have ever had is our mortgage. Every credit card is paid off 100% every month. Otherwise, we paid cash (or by credit card, which is paid off 100% every month) for everything, including vehicles.

Greatest threat to an individuals' wealth accumulation
Failure to begin and sustain a savings program (IRA, 401(k), etc.) at an early age.

(continued)

Favorite books
Life and Death in Shanghai (Nien Cheng); *Long Grey Line* (Rick Atkinson); *Wild Swans* (Jung Chang); *City of Joy* (Dominique Lapierre); *One Flew Over the Cuckoo's Nest* (Ken Kesey); *And the Band Played On* (Randy Shilts); *Fields of Fire* (Jim Webb). Every single book written by Ann Rule, starting with *The Stranger Beside Me.*

SIX *MORE* YEARS LATER ...
Net Worth Remained the Same

Retirement? Expecting expenses to slow down later in years. That was where we left Tom six years ago. He is still retired, again. Let's let him explain about the CFO job he took right before our last conversation.

"I was contacted by that US biotech start-up firm wanting me to become a CFO. I did that for about four years. They wanted to sell themselves, and I hired an investment banking firm, and they did wind up selling the company. I wasn't going to stay on; I had no intentions of staying on. So, as far as that goes, right now I am back to being retired."

So why retire again, and what was it like to go back to work? He describes it as more of "I am glad I tried it one more time, but I am ready to retire."

"I was almost 70. I had to drive 30 miles one way. The company needed me for a few years as they were undisciplined financially, whereas my background was very disciplined. I kind of brought them from point A to point B, and now that we're going from point B to point C, they needed someone with SEC-type experience. I did not have that expertise, nor did I want to learn it. I told them up front that if they sell the company and the company that buys it is listed on NASDAQ, I would retire and not compete for the CFO job at the new company. That's exactly what happened. So, it was my choice."

Let's dig down into the numbers. Tom had his money under management and wasn't taking any principal as income. He got some small equity in the bio-tech company that sold, but he doesn't consider that significant. Not touching the principal only lasted another 2–3 years after the last chat.

"After our last interview, I thought, 'Well, I don't have enough time to make it up; I may not have enough time to make it through another bear market. I was 100% in equities. I made the switch to a blend of fixed income and equity. My investment manager wasn't too keen on that.

"At that same time, my son went to work for TIA down in Charlotte. They were not accepting new members like Fisher Woods, Fidelity, Vanguard, or anyone else. But since he worked there, I could piggyback on him and have all my investments managed there. I did that. I meet with him about once a quarter.

"We set up a roughly 60/40 blend between fixed/equities. And we did that for quite a while until this spring, after the COVID thing, when the market fell fast. I decided to change it. I decided to flip-flop it to increase my equities and decrease my fixed income.

"I only did that because I kind of directed some ideas to my investment guy about where I wanted to put my money in a few months. For example, because I grew up in the oil industry and my father grew up in the oil industry, the price of oil and oil company stocks got hammered as well as the entire energy sector. So, I put some money into an energy ETF. And then I put some money into Vanguard Growth. And I did buy Berkshire B. It has worked out very well. The decision is: when do I revert to a more conservative approach? The 60/40 rule. I am watching the markets. These are very strange times."

Tom's income has adjusted. Being over 71, he is required to take minimum distributions from his IRA and is living quite comfortably off that with his social security. He also has a mortgage on his house that allows him to get some equity.

With his son now big in his financial business, Tom and he compare their strategies. "We know what we are doing, so he knows how much I have got. My daughter doesn't have any idea what my balance is. I am still of the opinion that whatever I leave them is a bonus. They can survive if I left them nothing, which won't happen unless I live to be 105."

A day in the life of Tom looks like waking up in the morning and not knowing what day of the week it is. He feels like it's the same routine. He gets up in the morning, reads the newspaper (on the internet), goes walking, and then piddles around the yard. In the evenings, they watch some Netflix series and basically relax. He does visit his daughter, who lives about two hours away about once a month for a four-day weekend. He loves his community. Williamsburg is where the Jamestown settlement was. It is a historic vacation spot the Rockefellers started in the 1950s. It is a retirement community.

"I have been mentoring American business school students for 15 years, and I always ask them, 'What is the biggest decision you have ever made in your life?' and 80% of the students say it was the decision to come to a school in America.

"That is my story as well, the decision between schools, which ended up with me attending a private college. When I was growing up in California in high school, I didn't know this until way after it happened, my junior year my dad's company wanted to transfer him to Alaska. He said, 'No, my son is about to be a senior, transfer me a year from now.' I finished there, and when I was looking for colleges, my dad wanted me to go to one of the small colleges in California. I wasn't all that excited to go into the California system.

"One day my English teacher was helping me write my college essays. We were talking, and I was complaining about not being excited about going to the California system and how I couldn't get into any other schools, as I did well in high school, but not the Stanford type of well. He said, 'How about Randolph-Macon College, Nashville, and Virginia?'"

"I never heard of it. Because, while I'm sure you haven't, that's where I went to school. It's all male; there are about 1,200 students. He gave me, back then, you could look through a paper catalog of this. They gave you the catalog, and I went home to my dad, handed it to him, and said, 'Well, what do you think about that?'

"He's from Virginia. But he knew at that time that he was going to be transferred to Oklahoma. So, from Oklahoma to California, or California to Virginia it is equidistant. It doesn't matter, travel-wise. The tuition for this private school was about $2,500 a year. And unbeknownst to a lot of people, when Ronald Reagan became governor of California, which was in the 1960s, one of the first things he did was charge out-of-state students tuition to go to the California system, which before that was tuition-free.

"As a result, the cost of attending a private school in Virginia versus staying in California was not significantly different. Dad said, 'Well, OK,' so I applied, and I got in.

"The big decision was to not go back to the California college but to go to a small private school in Virginia, which was huge. I mean, that changed my life. No doubt about it."

QUESTIONS FROM OUR OTHER MILLIONAIRES

Do you think you are rich?
Well, I don't worry about my next meal. I am not worried about losing my job or being furloughed. My income for the year is fixed. So, do I feel wealthy? Yeah, I guess I do. If I went to cash, I could live off of that for a long time.

What is important to you and how has that changed over time?
Our health. I think as you get older, you worry. I am positive, but that could change tomorrow. My daughter has figured out that when it comes time for us to be cared for, that will fall on her. She has said, "Why don't you move to Charlottesville and get settled here?" So, when it is time, we don't have to make any important decisions under stress. We have talked about it. For now, we are quite comfortable here.

How do you make important decisions?
Well, that now reminds me of a joke I have to tell. Johnny Carson had this couple on his show that was celebrating their 75th wedding anniversary. They were just as sharp as tacks. Johnny asked the husband, "What have you learned? What is the key to success?" Without batting an eye, the guy said, "Well, the day we were married, we made a decision that all the easy decisions would be made by me,

(continued)

and all the difficult things will be done by her. So far, we've never had a difficult decision."

It's hard for me to answer that question. I don't know that I had to make really difficult decisions. When I have a decision, I talk it over with my wife, you know, and together we come to some conclusions about what we want to do.

Quotes to Ruminate On

> **WHAT DO YOU THINK IS THE NEXT "BIG THING" AND TO WHAT PERSONAL CHARACTER TRAIT DO YOU ATTRIBUTE YOUR FINANCIAL SUCCESS?**

The winner is:
Energy Development – better ways of using natural resources, alternative energy, nuclear power

Very close second:
Biotech and Nanotech

Other notable mentions:
Significant gains in medical technology
Infrastructure, rebuilding the potable water systems
Wireless
Technology – melding of home and work technology

Consistently top mentioned traits:
- Perseverance; never giving up
- Have fun doing it; have a sense of humor
- Ability to assess risk
- Common sense
- Integrity

(continued)

- Confidence; courage to accomplish goals
- Learning from mistakes and adjusting quickly; being honest with yourself; recognizing your own limitations
- Willingness to take advice and do more research; learning behavior from others who have been successful
- Being able to work well with people at all levels; being a good communicator and team builder
- Ability to listen

CHAPTER 10

A Blank Piece of Paper with My Preferred Future

SKIP V.
Net Worth: $14 Million
Income: $250–300K
Started Investing: 21
Attained Millionaire Status: 44

Some people achieve their success through blind luck while some people create a road map. Skip, by and large, is part of the latter group. His success, he says, has come by identifying the characteristics of what he wants out of life and then waiting for the opportunities that fit. He attributes this mindset to his father who always told him, "Aim high and hold your aim."

Skip attended law school at a time when the Vietnam War was going on. He was eager and enthusiastic about signing up for the Marines and almost took a break from law school to do so. "The Marines had a program where you could sign up with the Marine Corps mid-law year, go to boot camp after your mid-law, but then go back and finish your senior year. I almost did that. In fact, I took the mental aptitude test and when the captain said, 'Let's go this way for your physical,' I hesitated and told him I wanted to think about it another day. I never went back and that decision to stay in school was one of the best things that ever happened to me."

After graduation he didn't even apply for a job because he *knew* he was going to go into the military. He was unmarried, he was A-1, but flunked the physical. "I had a bony growth on the inside of my shoulder blade where I couldn't move my arm back, or my shoulder back. They reclassified me to 1-Y. They weren't going to call me up, and I had a decision to make." Dealing with the sting of that rejection, he had to reevaluate what he wanted out of life.

He had a revelation that if he was going to work in the business world for the next 40-odd years, he better learn a thing or two about business. "I looked into a business school in Texas and found out they could waive a couple of classes for me, and I could double up and get out in 15 months. I was dating my wife-to-be, and that is what I did." Surprising to him, he ended up liking business more than law. In one sense he has used his law degree, but just never practiced law per se.

His father was a product of the Depression. He graduated from college through the grace of an aunt in 1932, and medical school in 1936, and he saw the worst of it. A key mantra his father always told him was, "Don't borrow money. Don't borrow money." Although he agreed in theory with the concept of living debt free, he didn't really understand or appreciate exactly what that meant.

However, he soon received a real-life lesson that made him regret not listening to his father. He was in the steel business early on and had decided it was better to have inventory on the floor than it was to have money in the bank. His steel inventory would appreciate rapidly 1–2% a month, as opposed to the money in the bank, which had a slower return.

That approach worked for him until one Tuesday morning when all the steel orders got canceled. "It kind of changed my approach to how a business should be run, especially a commodity business like steel.

"It brought home in spades to me what my dad was saying about not borrowing money. I think this concept applies to any business because it should be able to run so that it can survive the ups as well as the downs. Too many businesses try to shoot for the moon in the upturn and just do whatever they can to survive a downturn. Doing business with a long-term mentality, you have to be able to survive the downturns, because they are inevitable. So that was his lesson to me, and that is how I really learned it myself.

"I want to share something else about my father. My dad was a doctor. He was head of radiology at a hospital in Houston. But he had another practice with a doctor who was 15 years younger than he was, and I was 15 years younger than his partner. It would have been a logical progression, if you will, if I had gone into the family business of medicine. But I am already a 'Jr.,' and I didn't want to be just a Jr. I wanted to do something else. The only advice my dad gave me when I was a young man, about 15 years old, about what to do business wise was: 'Don't be a doctor.'

"I don't know if his advice was good or not, but his reasoning was impeccable. His reasoning, and this was in 1958, was, 'The government is starting to get into my business. And it is going to get more into my business.' That is why he told me not to become a doctor, and it is truly incredible what has happened."

Skip never had a burning desire to do anything specific. When he got out of school, he didn't know what he wanted to do. He decided if he went into consulting, he could see a variety of businesses. His first job out of school was with the consulting practice of one of the, then Big 8 accounting firms. "For the first six months, I went out on one project and spent a lot of time in rooms with a lot of people, just looking at each other. I finally went into the head of the office and said, 'This is just not working. I have got to work. This is driving me crazy. I am either going to work here or somewhere else.' He ended up switching me to the tax department. I never found that stimulating. Tax returns were done by hand back then, and I did *a lot* of state returns by hand.

"My third year with the firm I got to go to New York and work in the office of one of the senior partners. I am really glad I did, although the assignment was not as advertised."

It was there he learned how a firm operates from the inside. He learned the fears and concerns, as well as the things that did well.

"One lesson I certainly learned from my time there is that you really want to be in the headquarters of any operation. When I was in Houston, the man in charge of the operation and all the offices in the southwest region was looked upon as wonderful, God-like, etc. What I found in the senior office in New York is that man didn't really count for anything there. The only ones that seemed to really matter were the partners in New York." It was a good lesson to him, that if you are going to be with a large organization you want to be at the center of the activity, not out in the hinterlands.

He reminisces of those few years in New York City. He and his wife decided to live right in Manhattan and took advantage of New York

City as tourists and enjoyed it immensely. It was a great experience for them, but the work experience left something to be desired.

Shortly after he left Houston, he had been contacted by a man to come work for his company there, and so he returned to Texas to become financial assistant to the president and moved on to the CFO of a company being put on the New York Stock Exchange. He was 33 years old and CFO for five and a half years.

"The last 6–12 months I was there, there were things that should have been done – I used to say as obvious as a nose on a goat – that needed to be done business-wise. The president was not interested in doing anything. I have referred to it as almost being a plantation. He just took care of everything. I saw the other vice presidents not pushing very hard because there was nothing they could do to influence the position because the president just stated his own position. Once again, I didn't like it."

Skip then got recruited by a drilling company and considered it good timing. Not even two months after he was there, the firm was sold to a larger company, but he turned that experience into something positive. "Being newly unemployed, I realized it was a wonderful opportunity to do whatever I wanted to do next. I had spent 90% of my time saying 'You know, isn't it awful, etc.' The challenge for me was to figure out what it was that I wanted to do."

Skip wrote down on paper what he would like to do next.

He didn't focus on the job, but instead listed the characteristics of the position he wanted to have, what kind of people he wanted to work with, what kind of organization, where, what kind of compensation, etc. He never sent out a batch of résumés but took that sheet of paper and shared it with some people that he trusted and respected.

It was just a month after that he got a call from one of those people about an introduction that ended up being his next great opportunity. "It fit hand in glove with what I had identified as exactly what I wanted to do. I wanted to run a business. That was one of the reasons I left the first job. I wanted to be chief operating officer. I wanted to have some equity opportunity with an upside. I wanted to be in Houston. The proposal was I would come on as COO from day one, with the idea of putting together a management group. And somewhere from three to five years, the management group would buy the company from the family.

"That is one of those rare times in life that worked out just as we discussed it at the beginning. Four years later, five of us in management bought the business. I had the majority interest. The families were happy because they had a succession plan, and they had a way to get liquidity for them and their estates.

"I learned yet again to write down my goals and not to dwell on why I'm unhappy. Any time I've carefully thought about and then written down my goals, they have always happened."

The next 20 years were spent as a partner in an investment banking firm. He and his partner didn't take salaries or require large monthly retainers, which most companies did to cover their overhead. They kept the expenses low in order to show a certain level of commitment, an emotional commitment, to the client and to develop lasting relationships.

In working with their clients, pursuant to a written agreement, they did receive a small monthly retainer, which was important to keep the lights on, but also important to show a certain level of commitment for the client – from the client to them, and emotional commitment from the firm to the client. Their take-home pay came when they accomplished their client's objectives, whether it was to buy, sell, or finance.

"When that happened, we got a nice contingent fee, and that's when our partners would sit down and divide up the money. So those were the special hits as opposed to salaries and you just didn't know when the next one was going to happen."

Most of Skip's net worth is in real estate, but he is trying to see it go into more liquid assets. He spends about $250,000 a year and his income is from his principal and some royalties.

"I think the way we accumulated wealth was not by saving per se, but by hits. What I mean by that is like a bonus or a nice year in the business or selling the business. My observation is that if you're on a salary where you have kind of a level, hopefully an upward level, of income, your lifestyle gets adjusted to take care of that where certainly some could be saved, but not a really meaningful amount. That has been my experience."

His first liquidity event came with the business the management team bought from the family. He sold that business and then did the same thing again at $2 million. "I thought, once again, about what I really wanted to do next. I had a wonderful opportunity. The logical thing was to go find another business to invest in and do it again. I had worked really hard on it and then worked hard on the investment banking firm." He didn't take a salary for 20 years in that model. It may be the next big hit.

When Skip reached his fifties, he started feeling a need for better balance in his life. "Work has always been important to me. Let me give you an example. When I went to work at that family business, the largest product that they had was galvanized steel. I didn't know what 'galvanized' meant. I had to go to the dictionary and see what it meant. But I've always worked hard, partly out of concern. I didn't want to fail. I wanted to do the best that I could.

"I found out at that job pretty early that if I worked on Saturdays I could get twice as much done as I could any day of the week. And then I found out I could get twice as much done on Sundays compared to Saturday, which would be four times a week day. I was working seven days a week. Nobody was at the office on Sunday. Saturday there were a few people there, but not that many. And finally my wife said, 'I don't think this is working.' So, I changed, and instead of working at the office on Sunday, I brought my work home and worked at home on Sunday. And she said, 'No, this is not what I had in mind either.' There were times in my personal life where I felt like I needed work, but I began to see that I needed more balance."

And guess what? This idea of balance began when he took a sheet of paper and divided it into three parts of how he spent his time. How much time did he spend on business, how much on social, and how much on personal time. Then he made another circle in parts on how he *would like* to spend his time.

They were quite different and brought home to him the feeling that had been growing about wanting better balance in life.

Years later – you know where this is going – he once again sat down and used those two lists to type up his preferred future. "It brought out those thoughts that had been rolling around in my mind for the past years. Associated thoughts. I had close to two pages of single-spaced thoughts. I went back the next day, and I organized all those into topics. I have gone back to that piece of paper somewhere between 50 and 100 times just to remind myself where I'm going.

"I view it as a work in progress, something never to be completed. Always looking to my preferred future, and always being able to refine it, as I may hear something from somebody. I may have a new thought. Circumstances might change. For instance, my mom was an important topic on my list, as you can imagine. Mom died a few years ago, and now that large topic is down to 'Have good thoughts about your Mom.'

"Because of that document I knew I was going to be leaving the investment banking firm. I shared that with my partner three years before I left, so he knew what was happening in my mind. I kept him informed.

"An example of the flow was: Would I like to stay where I was in that office? No. Would I like to office at home? No. Where would I like to office? I would like to office at the building by our house. Would I like to office with somebody else, and if so, with whom? I would like to office with a friend who started out as a business friend. From this list I ended up taking a friend to lunch and asking if he would like to office together. And he was delighted."

SIX *MORE* YEARS LATER ...
Net Worth Increased to $15.5 Million

JOHN: All right, Skip, you were an investment banker, and then the floor fell out of the markets after our first conversation. What happened to you?

SKIP: Let me tell you the good news. Well, you remember the time when everything started to go to hell in a handbasket. I had been planning for some time to leave investment banking and I had kept my partner informed. About a year before I did so, we brought in another partner. Then as I was leaving, we brought in another partner. I left in September 2007. How is that for good timing?

JOHN: That is exceptionally good timing. And another big hit for you.

SKIP: In hindsight, if I had been able to pick my date, I don't think I could have done it better.

JOHN: But you had money in the market, so what happened to that money?

SKIP: It dipped like everyone else's. It went down the same percentage. I don't think my financial advisor was any better than anyone else's financial advisor. The good news for me was, looking at my net worth, way too much of it was in real estate and raw land. I had been working toward selling land and getting a much better balance of liquidity. One very important tract had a contract on it, but of course that fell apart. It stayed, but fortunately there was no debt on it. Then Houston has been booming the last five years. A year and a half ago, things got hot, and I was able to get pretty good competition for this tract. I ended up selling it for twice what it had been under contract for the five or six years before.

JOHN: That is a pretty good compound for holding over that time.

SKIP: It was wonderful because instead of being liquid in 2007 and riding the market down with all my chips in, the majority of the chips were literally set aside because I couldn't sell the real estate. However, the real estate came back wonderfully, so that is my good news.

JOHN: That is good news. So, your net worth is up somewhat from where it was?

SKIP: It is probably up a spot from $15 million. The good news is that most of it is liquid. I think that is good news, because I feel better.

JOHN: Liquid in that you are heavily in the market now?

SKIP: I am in the market now, but I am heavily spread out in the market. Pockets here and pockets there. As of right now, I am in a fairly defensive position. I am concerned about what the next year or two will bring in the market. I personally think there is more downside risk than upside risk.

JOHN: Are you planning to once again ride it out, or are you going to have more judicious timing this time?

SKIP: A certain amount of it is in a structured deal where if the market goes down too much, I'm getting out of it. I am not going to ride it down for an extended amount of months. The last time I rode it down, I had a much higher percentage in equities than I probably should have for my age.

This time I have a much better balance. A certain amount is defensive in terms of bonds and things of that nature.

TIFFANI: Where are you getting your income from now?

SKIP: Still off of investments, about $250,000 to $300,000 per year. That is dividends and interest and whatever the appreciation is.

JOHN: I want to touch more on your dad; he kept stressing no debt to you.

SKIP: Yes, he was a product of the Depression, being born in 1910. He lived through it, and he told me to not go into debt. At that time, I mentioned I was in the steel business and it was more valuable to have steel on the floor than money in the bank because steel was appreciating fast. That was all very true until about 10:30 on a Tuesday morning and all the orders got canceled. That was a learning curve for me. Dad got a lot smarter that day. So, I tried to live my life after that with no debt and I feel a whole lot better about it.

TIFFANI: How do you spend your time nowadays? Is it much different?

SKIP: A little more detail of how I have refined my "preferred future." I had been having feelings of change building up over time. The thing was when I left investment banking, what I wanted to do – if I had my choice – was I wanted to share an office with the smartest, most hard-working guy I knew. And that happened. I wanted to have the lady who was our office manager and my assistant to run our office and I wanted to be in the River Oaks Bank Building. I asked my assistant if she would like to leave and work for me and this other guy and she said yes. The hardest thing was getting into the River Oaks Bank Building, but we got in. So, I had a nice transition from investment banking with a great office partner with a great woman running the office. I asked her to come into my office, as seriously as I could. She was a little nervous and sat on the edge of her chair. I asked her how she would like to work for us. She kind of looked at me, and squeaked, "Who else is there?" We just got up and hugged, and hugged and cried. She said, "I have been praying for this; this is exactly what I have been praying for."

Now I have great flexibility. Someone asked me if I was retired, and I said I have an office that I go to every day and I work every day. They finally asked me what I did, and I said, "Whatever I want to."

TIFFANI: So, what has been added to that preferred future horizon?

SKIP: I am looking to improve my golf game. I want to shoot my age and I almost did this summer. I need to shoot a 72, but I had a 74 and a 75. I am doing that. It's amazing how many things there are to do. I love reading and keeping up with all the Mauldin reports and things of that nature. At this point in time, I have no responsibilities to anyone else. I am literally just doing what I want to do.

JOHN: So, in a sense, you have chosen the classic retirement.

SKIP: I don't know what retirement is. All I know is I don't do what I used to do. I still feel a need to go into the office to get out of the house. I have all my stuff there. I don't have a feeling of the need to work for a check, so in that sense you are right.

JOHN: So you are comfortable with the way the markets are going and the way you've hedged yourself so that you won't have to worry about that again in the future?

SKIP: I hope that is true. I figured out a long time ago that I don't know enough or have enough time to do my own investing. When I was in law school, the first two years I made $25,000 trading with a buddy of mine who was a broker. My last year in law school, I lost $25,000. And I didn't do anything differently, it was just timing. The only person who made money was him, which is fine, but what I learned was that it wasn't because of my smarts that I made that money. I was just the cork on the water, and it happened to go up or it happened to go down. I turn it over to the professionals and I'm comfortable with how and why it's invested. I look at the monthly reports and not much more. My money manager and I talked for an hour yesterday. We periodically do that.

TIFFANI: Do you have a will and trust set up, and how do your kids understand your financial situation?

SKIP: Yes I do. I shared my portfolio, where we are, and our net worth with all our kids. I think they are of an age and a maturity where they can understand this information. I think it is important for them to see and know.

TIFFANI: After all this, what could have been the most likely thing to have kept you from achieving your success?

SKIP: Getting stuck in the middle, continuing the status quo. When unhappy in a job, I focus on the characteristics of what I would like and put them down on paper – don't dwell on why you are unhappy when you set goals; when I have, they have always happened. A significant key to happiness is always wanting to learn.

What personal character trait do you attribute to your success?
Strong work ethic – when I asked my wife she said, "Good listener, analytical, making a plan and staying with it."

Stupidest thing you spent money on
Nothing jumps out at me other than buying a too-small pair of canary yellow loafers from Norton-Ditto because they were only $6.00.

Favorite books
Animal Farm (George Orwell); *Cypress Point Club* (Alister MacKenzie); and books on World War II – Asia and the Pacific.

SIX *MORE* YEARS LATER ...
Net Worth Increased Substantially

The emerging themes coming through in these connections have a similar vein. A lot of our millionaires have moments in their lives when they make a decision, or create a value system, and that seems to direct the flow of the course of their lives. Skip had at least three times, he has told us about, where he wrote down on paper what he wanted to do, what his business would look like, then he saw the opportunity that matched. When he reached his fifties, he sat down again and divided his life into sections – how he was spending his time and how he wanted to spend his time – and then he adjusted his life. He knew it would be a work in progress, that there would be opportunities to refine it. We checked back in to find out if he is still refining his list, and if he has the balance he wrote down as a goal.

"Tiffani, I am comfortable where I am right now. Any life lessons I learned the first few times I changed jobs. I had focused primarily on why I wanted to leave where I was, what I didn't like about what I was doing or the situation, or whether I was unhappy, although that certainly overstates it. I focused less on what else I might do in the future.

"I always asked, what would it be if I could write the script? I spent a couple of hours typing, and I came up with what I wanted to do in the situation I would like to get myself into. I've probably used that same approach three times now, and I now have a fantastic arrangement as a result. And I did that several years ago, I guess it worked out.

"Where I'm going with that is, if I were talking with a young person and giving them one piece of advice, it would be for them to focus on what they want to do, not necessarily job-wise, because that's hard to know. But what kind of characteristics do you want in that position? What kind of people do you want to work with? Where do you want to work? What kind of business do you want to be in? And the closer you can get to get that down on paper in my mind, the better the chances are that that's the kind of position you're going to end up in.

"I'm in that position right now. Last we talked I had written down what I wanted to do next. That was the office.

"This building I am in, there are others there, a lot of guys like me who just wanted an office and went in there. They kind of died with their boots on. Now that was years ago, I work with the smartest guy and have the best woman working for us. We have only had one disagreement. There is one thing we don't agree on, and that is who is the most fortunate, who is the luckiest? Nobody will give in."

Well, Skip, what does the day look like, going into this office? He says that he reads a lot. (Don't ask his wife, as she will tell you he doesn't read – what she means is he doesn't read books). He reads a lot on the computer. He chases golf balls and exercises. In terms of business, he has his financial advisor. Someone asked him, "Are you retired?" His response? "Listen, I said I have an office; I go to the office every day and I work every day. I enjoy current events. As an undergraduate, I majored in history, which I think is an interesting major that gives you a good perspective on the world. And I like staying up with current events, and sharing thoughts. So that's what I do. The last time I worked for my money was 13 years ago."

Skip and his wife have three children whom they are incredibly proud of, and they are still aware of the financial success of their parents. "They are good people, very proud. My wife and I take pride in that. We have been able to share with them in a tax-efficient way. We've shared liquid assets in the form of cash, or near cash for $3–4 million, and in assets another $3 million.

"Some of it is in real estate interests and limited partnerships. In years when things were not as good, we could get a pretty reasonable valuation and because of that we haven't had to pay the gift tax.

"Life is good. You've inquired about my penchant for spending money. We have a very nice house here in Durango, on the river. You go to the edge and look down at the river. And it's just so peaceful and delightful, I just can't tell you; it's in a forest. And then we have a nice townhouse in Houston. We're in the process of relocating to a mid-rise six blocks away from where we currently live and a block and a half away from the Liberal Bank building, where I work."

And ... drum roll ... the numbers. Skip's net worth has increased from six years ago, even after giving those extensive gifts to his children. His income still comes from his dividends, interest, and appreciation.

In terms of allocation, he is very conservative, he has a lot of cash at this point. One of those reasons is that if they don't sell the townhouse he mentioned, he wants to have enough money to buy a condo in a mid-rise building in Houston (they prefer a place with no stairs which the mid-rise would have versus the condo).

The investment part of his portfolio is currently about 8% equity, 22% fixed income, and 30% alternative investments, with 8% of that in gold. The rest is in cash. He feels comfortable with it, and if he tripled his net worth, it wouldn't change his lifestyle one iota.

QUESTIONS FROM OUR OTHER MILLIONAIRES

Do you think you are rich?
I feel comfortable. I don't have financial concerns. I am very fortunate; I don't feel like I have pressure points in my life. I mean, if it were a $500 million lottery, would that change how I live now? Only one thing I can think of: I would never fly commercial again.

What is important to you and how has that changed over time?
I think one thing is being comfortable with myself. And I do feel comfortable with myself. When I was younger, I didn't necessarily feel comfortable with myself from the point of view of competence, knowledge, and things like that. I don't have the challenges now that I had when I was younger, in terms of business, performance, and effectiveness. I had more financial difficulties back then, as well as more difficulties with having children. And right now, I mean, I've got to be knocking on wood. But as I said earlier, I don't have a pressure point, including with myself. I have a clear conscience.

Insight Journal

Create Your Own Story: What do you love to do? What have you done that has been the most satisfying? What activities have always been easy for you that may be difficult for others? What do most people compliment you on? What was your best "mistake"? What would you do differently knowing what you know now? If you connected with something, put yourself in that situation, think about what would you have done or not done, and follow that imaginary path. If something gave you a bad taste in your mouth, consider why and what choices you would make differently.

Look back at what stood out to you, what you highlighted.

What were your "aha" moments? Don't lose the inspiration. Write it down now.

INDEX

Page numbers followed by *f* refer to figures.